How to Prepare for

The Coming Global Crisis

A Spiritual Survival Guide

by Marvin Moore

Pacific Press® Publishing Association
Nampa, Idaho
Oshawa, Ontario, Canada

This book was
Edited by Tim Lale
Copyedited by Wendy Perla
Cover photo/illustration by Ian Lawrence/Photonica

ISBN 0-8163-1798-4

00 01 02 03 04 • 5 4 3 2 1

Contents

CHAPTER

Crisis

Dawn was an omen of how the day would end, though neither Lois nor I had any way of knowing this. Gray mornings are not unusual in north-central Texas. Most of the time nobody takes them that seriously. But by noon, life had changed forever for both of us, especially for Lois.

My cousin Robert had picked us up the night before at the Dallas/Fort Worth airport and taken us to his home out in the country, not far from the little town of Joshua, twenty minutes south of Fort Worth. My mother had died the day after Christmas in 1996, and we had flown in from Idaho for her funeral.

We never made it.

Since the funeral wasn't till 2:00 in the afternoon the day after we arrived, Lois and I slept in a bit later than usual that morning. After breakfast Lois said, "I'm going on a walk. I'll be back in an hour." I'd have gone with her, except that I still had to finish preparing my funeral sermon. I pecked away at my computer till I had finished outlining what I wanted to say. About an hour had passed by then, and I remember looking at my watch and wondering when Lois would return. Ten minutes later I was beginning to get a bit worried, but I have a habit of worrying any time Lois doesn't show up when I expect her to, so I tried to put the anxiety out of my mind.

Then the phone rang.

By the end of December the weather is quite cold in north-central Texas. The temperature was probably in the forties when Lois left on her walk, so she wore a long, brown, quilted coat. The winding country road was paved but desolate. Lois doesn't remember seeing anyone driving by in either direction the entire time she walked away from Robert's home.

She'd been walking almost half an hour when she passed a large fenced yard. Four large pit bull dogs charged toward the fence, snarling and barking ferociously. *It's a good thing they're behind that fence,* Lois thought. But a moment later one of them wiggled through a hole at the bottom of the fence, and soon all four dogs were charging toward her.

"Jesus, help me! Jesus, help me!" Lois screamed. But the dogs charged on. They knocked her to the ground and tore the coat from her body. Lois heard the grinding sound as one of the dogs gnawed on her skull, and she felt the pain as the others chewed on her arms, hands, and legs. She put her hand to her forehead, and it felt sticky. Looking at it, she saw blood. *I'm going to die here on this desolate country road,* she thought. Yet somehow she wasn't afraid. A moment later she lost consciousness.

When she woke up, the dogs were gone, and she heard a man's voice.

"Can you stand up?"

Lois struggled, but she couldn't stand. Then she felt a pair of strong arms lift her and carry her a few feet to a pickup. Morgan Halbert laid her gently in the bed of his truck. Lois looked up and saw a woman standing beside the pickup. "Lindsey," the man said, "I think you should stay in the back with this woman while I drive to town."

Lindsey Halbert knelt beside Lois and took her hand. "What's your name?" she asked. Lois told her. "And where's your home?"

"I'm from Idaho."

"Where are you staying?"

"With Robert Hadley."

Lindsey knew Robert. She kept Lois talking all the way to Joshua.

Every bump in the road sent pain shooting through Lois's body, but each one also took her farther from those terrible dogs. She was alive, and she was on the way to help.

I picked up the phone on the second ring. A woman's voice said, "Is this Mr. Moore?"

"Yes, it is."

"Mr. Moore, I'm calling from the Joshua police station. Your wife has just been attacked by four pit bull dogs, and she's in bad shape. An ambulance is on the way. You'd better get down here right away."

I threw the phone back on the hook and yelled at Robert. He let me drive. Fortunately, Joshua is only about five minutes from Robert's house— at least at the speed I drove. I slammed on the brakes in front of the police station and jumped out of the car. A police officer sat in the bed of the pickup caring for Lois. Her face was covered with blood. A moment later the ambulance drove up, and two EMTs took over. I sat up front with the ambulance driver on the way to Fort Worth.

Lois spent a couple of hours in surgery and four days in the Intensive Care Unit of John Peter Smith Hospital. Then the doctors let her fly back home. United Airlines was extremely accommodating. They put us in first class at no extra charge, and they arranged for an EMT to change Lois's dressings between planes in Denver.

The major damage was on the calf of Lois's right leg. One of the dogs had torn away a strip of muscle and veins and flesh almost three inches wide and half an inch deep running most of the way around her leg. After a skin graft came the long road to recovery. The first time Lois tried walking outside, it took her forty-five minutes to go two doors down the street and back with the aid of a walker.

Because the doctors at the hospital in Fort

Worth did not want to stretch the injury, they had allowed her to develop a severe foot drop, and the only way to get range of motion back was to do the exercises that her physical therapist had recommended. The pain was excruciating, but Lois gritted her teeth and pushed ahead. I was amazed at how hard she worked. And her progress was rapid at first. On one visit the physical therapist encouraged her to set a goal of regaining an inch from her foot drop during the following week, and she made it!

But the struggle was as much spiritual as it was physical. *Why, God? Why me?* she thought. *Where were You when those dogs attacked? Why didn't You stop them?*

One morning during her devotional time, Lois read the story of Jesus healing the man at the pool of Bethesda who'd been crippled for 38 years. "God," she cried, "am I going to be a cripple the rest of my life? I can't handle that"—and she redoubled her effort. But by now her foot had regained about all it was going to from the foot drop, and progress stopped.

"The basic struggle was control," Lois says. "Who was in charge of my recovery, anyway? More important, who was in charge of my life? I finally came to the place I had to say to God, 'If You want me to be a cripple the rest of my life, that's OK.' " Fortunately, today she is able to walk quite normally. But that surrender, she now says, was one of the hardest things she ever did.

THE COMING GLOBAL CRISIS

Lois experienced a crisis. We all experience crises from time to time. There is no such thing as life without them. The issue is not *whether* we'll experience crises but *how*. Will we be ready for them, or won't we? And I'm not talking about whether we'll have enough money to handle them. Often, money isn't even an issue. But spirituality always is. In every crisis, *the most important issue is our spirituality*, because the quality of our spirituality at the moment a crisis strikes determines how we will handle it.

I'd like to state right now a principle about spirituality and crisis that we will be looking at over and over again throughout this book:

A crisis is both a test of our present spirituality
and a springboard into a deeper spirituality.

Lois may not have felt like it, but she actually *was* ready for this crisis. She had maintained a program of meditation and spiritual study for years. Much of that study was from the world's most spiritually powerful book—the Bible. For several years she'd also been active in a Twelve-Step recovery program that had helped her to accept responsibility for her character defects and follow a systematic spiritual plan for dealing with them.

Being ready for a crisis doesn't mean that you necessarily breeze through it with no pain. It means you have the tools to handle it without being devastated by it. It means you have developed enough spiritual maturity to respond wisely instead of recklessly. You may blame God at first. You may despair over the future. You may feel bitter toward those who were responsible for your pain. Spiritual preparation means you'll have the inner wisdom and strength to maintain your trust in God. It means you'll eventually come to the place you can forgive those who could have prevented your pain—who may even have caused it. And you'll be a better person for it.

Once, when I was in the middle of one of the worst crises of my life, a friend said to me, "Marvin, remember that a crisis is a dangerous opportunity."

He's right. If we handle it properly, a crisis is an outstanding opportunity for spiritual growth and possibly even for material growth as well. However, it's also dangerous because if we blow it, we may be worse off than before. And how we handle it depends more than anything else on the level of spiritual growth we have experienced at the time the crisis strikes.

Lois's encounter with the dogs and the recovery process that followed was a severe test of the spirituality she'd been developing over the years. It also launched her into a deeper spirituality than she had ever experienced before, which, perhaps, is why God allowed the crisis to happen.

Neither Lois nor I know what crisis we may

face in the future, but we're sure of one thing: Both of us, and especially Lois, will be better prepared for the next major crisis in our lives because of the spiritual growth we gained from the last one.

The next crisis in your life could be personal— just you or you and members of your family. You or your spouse might lose your job, one of you might come down with a life-threatening cancer, or you might discover that one of your children is a drug addict. Will you be ready? Spiritually, I mean.

Sometimes, however, crisis can strike an entire community of people. Many community crises are the result of a natural disaster such as a tornado or a devastating drought. However, it's also a community crisis when a major company shuts down, leaving many people jobless. Will you be ready? Spiritually, I mean.

Some crises are even global. The world experienced at least three such crises during the twentieth century—two world wars and one major depression. And during most of the second half of the century, the Cold War kept the world in fear of a global nuclear holocaust.

Nobody knows when the next global crisis will hit the world. All we can be sure of is that there will be one someday. The question is, Will you and I be ready?

Spiritually, I mean.

CHAPTER 2

Global Crisis

Did you breathe a sigh of relief on January 1, 2000? Perhaps you should have—and I'm not talking about Y2K. Notice the following predictions by psychics and prophets, some modern, and some not so modern, that were supposed to have been fulfilled during the latter part of the 1990s:

- **Nostradamus:** Antichrist will appear on Manhattan Island in 1999.
- **Jeanne Dixon:** World War III will break out in 1999.
- **Edgar Cayce:** The earth will shift on its axis near the end of the second millennium, bringing about worldwide earthquakes, volcanoes, and tidal waves.
- **Ruth Montgomery:** Shortly before 2000 the earth will shift on its axis, causing global natural disasters. But certain enlightened people will be rescued by spaceships sent from a more enlightened planet.
- **An Indian prophecy:** A white buffalo calf will be born on the farm of white people, after

which terrible natural disasters will occur within five years. (On August 20, 1994 a white buffalo was born on a farm in Janesville, Wisconsin.)

- **The Virgin Mary:** During the late 1990s, fire will descend from heaven, wiping out a great part of humanity. A chastisement worse than the Flood of Noah will come upon the world.

Now that January 1, 2000 has come and gone, you know that nothing like that happened during the late 1990s. In case you failed to breathe that sigh of relief on January 1, you can go ahead and let it out now.

If you believe the prognosticators, you'd better hold your breath just a bit longer:

- **The great pyramid:** Students of the monumental structure claim that its architects built into its labyrinths a prediction that Doomsday will come in September 2001.
- **Berosus:** The second-century Chaldean philosopher allegedly proclaimed that the world will end in October 2001.
- **Howard Furness:** Earth will pass through a cloud of comets in 2000, bringing a rain of comets and asteroids that will destroy most life forms on our planet.
- **Richard Noone:** On May 5, 2000 the sun and moon and all the planets will line up, exerting a tremendous gravitational pull on planet

Earth. The South Pole ice cap will shift, sending trillions of tons of ice to the equator.
- **Gordon Michael Scallion:** A Hopi Indian prophecy predicts that a new sun will enter our solar system between 1998 and 2001, bringing terrible natural disasters. Boulder, Colorado will become Atlantic beach front property.

Most of these predictions share one thing in common: Global natural disasters on the scale of Noah's Flood will devastate our planet, bringing about the end of the world, or at least of civilization, as we know it.

The majority of people probably treat prognostications such as these with a smile and a shrug. I tend to do so myself, particularly given the abysmal fulfillment rate of the annual predictions published by the likes of *The Globe, The Sun,* and *The National Enquirer.*

However, another source of information is available that I trust far more than I do these scandal sheets. And while it doesn't set dates, this other source of information matches the best (or the worst) of the dire predictions the tabloids throw at us.

Yes, I'm talking about the Bible. Let's start with the ancient prophet Daniel:

> "At that time Michael, the great prince who protects your people, will arise. There will be a time of distress

such as has not happened from the beginning of nations until then."[1]

Daniel didn't say anything in this brief paragraph about natural disasters. He just said that a time of terrible global distress is coming, with no cause mentioned. So does that mean we're in the dark? Do we have no idea *from the Bible* about what's coming?

Let's look at a couple of other Old Testament writers. Here's how Joel described the weeks and months leading up to the end of the world:

> "I will show wonders in the heavens and on the earth, blood and fire and billows of smoke. The sun will be turned to darkness and the moon to blood before the coming of the great and dreadful day of the Lord."[2]

The "great and dreadful day of the Lord" is Old Testament code language for "the end of the world," which Christians generally identify with the second coming of Christ. And notice what Joel said would happen *before* that time:

- Wonders in the heavens.
- On the earth blood and fire and billows of smoke.
- The sun turned to darkness.
- The moon turned to blood.

Global Crisis

This is more of an impressionistic word picture than it is a description of anything we can make sense of. But the impression is clearly ominous. A number of possibilities exist for creating Joel's "blood and fire and billows of smoke": Volcanoes, nuclear warfare, regional forest fires, and asteroids or comets come to mind. And perhaps the sun turning dark and the moon turning blood red, besides expanding on Joel's "wonders in the heavens," are related to his "billows of smoke." Whatever the cause, the question is, What would human life be like if Joel's ominous picture were to be fulfilled literally?

Before answering that question, let's look next at a couple of prophecies by the Old Testament prophet Isaiah:

> See, the day of the Lord is coming
>   a cruel day, with wrath and fierce anger—
> to make the land desolate
>   and destroy the sinners within it.
> The stars of heaven and their constellations
>   will not show their light.
> The rising sun will be darkened
>   And the moon will not give its light. . . .
> I will make man scarcer than pure gold,
>   more rare than the gold of Ophir.
> Therefore I will make the heavens tremble;
>   and the earth will shake from its place
> at the wrath of the Lord Almighty,
>   in the day of his burning anger.[3]

THE COMING GLOBAL CRISIS

Like Joel, Isaiah is talking about "the day of the Lord"—what we today would call "the end of the world." And how does Isaiah describe it?

- The land is desolate.
- The stars of heaven and their constellations refuse to shine.
- The sun and moon are darkened.
- Human beings are more scarce than gold.
- The heavens tremble, and the earth shakes from its place.

Not a pleasant picture! In addition to the darkening of the sun, moon, and stars, Isaiah says that during the days just before the end of the world the land will be desolate, human beings will have practically become an extinct species, and there will be terrible earthquakes. And Isaiah has more to say:

> Terror and pit and snare await you,
>   O people of the earth. . . .
> The floodgates of the heavens are opened,
>   the foundations of the earth shake.
> The earth is broken up,
>   the earth is split asunder,
>   the earth is thoroughly shaken.
> The earth reels like a drunkard,
>   it sways like a hut in the wind.[4]

Sounds like those psychic predictions of the

earth shifting on its axis, doesn't it? And that's just the Old Testament. Let's take a look at the New Testament. We'll begin with words from Jesus Himself, first as recorded by Matthew, then by Luke:

Matthew

"Immediately after the distress of those days
'the sun will be darkened,
and the moon will not give its light;
the stars will fall from the sky,
and the heavenly bodies will be shaken.' "[5]

Luke

"There will be signs in the sun, moon and stars. On the earth, nations will be in anguish and perplexity at the roaring and tossing of the sea. Men will faint from terror, apprehensive of what is coming on the world, for the heavenly bodies will be shaken."[6]

Notice that in Matthew's version, Jesus' description of falling stars and darkening of the sun and moon is an echo of Isaiah. In fact, most commentators agree that He's quoting Isaiah, though the quotation is admittedly loose. And Luke informs us that these signs in the heavens will cause global anguish and perplexity and throw the human race into a panic. Some students of prophecy have suggested that perhaps Jesus' prediction of falling stars will be fulfilled by comets and asteroids. If you've read your newspaper at all in the last few years or followed the news on TV, you know that comets and asteroids could indeed cause the kind of global panic that Jesus predicted.

And now notice these words of Jesus, again speaking of the final days of earth's history.

> "For then there will be great dis-
> tress, unequaled from the beginning
> of the world until now—and never to
> be equaled again. If those days had not
> been cut short, no one would survive,
> but for the sake of the elect those days
> will be shortened."[7]

Please notice: The time of distress that is com-ing on our planet will be so severe that if God didn't cut it short, *no one would survive.* In other words, the human race will be in great danger of becoming the next extinct species. Jesus was predicting a crisis so severe that it will have the potential of wiping the human race off the planet. That's as bad as anything the psychics ever thought of predicting!

And there's more. Here's what John predicted in Revelation:

> Then there came flashes of light-
> ning, rumblings, peals of thunder and
> a severe earthquake. No earthquake

like it has ever occurred since man has been on earth, so tremendous was the quake. . . . Every island fled away and the mountains could not be found.[8]

Any earthquake powerful enough to flatten all the mountains and make the islands disappear under the ocean is one mighty earthquake! It sounds every bit as bad as those psychic predictions of the earth shifting on its axis. *But this time the Bible predicted it, not the psychics!*

If the Bible is correct—and I believe it is—then sometime in the future, our planet will face a crisis of massive proportions. Not just you and your family. Not just your city or even your country, but the entire globe. Furthermore, I believe these events are very likely to happen in your lifetime and mine. *The world is moving toward its final crisis.*

The following chapter describes the spiritual challenges you and I will encounter during earth's final crisis, and then we'll talk about how to prepare to meet them.

---

[1]Daniel 12:1.
[2]Joel 2:30, 31.
[3]Isaiah 13:9-13.
[4]Isaiah 24:17-20.
[5]Matthew 24:29.
[6]Luke 21:25, 26.
[7]Matthew 24:21, 22.
[8]Revelation 16:18, 20.

Global Spiritual Crisis

The word *sin* has fallen into considerable disrepute in our society. To some people the whole idea is a big joke. Many of our popular entertainers laugh about sin and the conservative religious people who talk about it.

Yet even the most nonreligious person recognizes that certain behaviors are so totally reprehensible that they cannot be tolerated by a civil society. And a word that defines such behavior, which is acceptable to all parties, does exist. We call it *evil*.

For nearly 60 years now, our culture has viewed Hitler as the embodiment of evil and Auschwitz as the ultimate symbol of evil. One newspaper report called Hitler "so gross, so infernal a figure, he threatens a fundamental law among writers: that no subject is forbidden."[1]

Unfortunately, Hitler and Auschwitz are not anomalies in our world. People similar to Hitler have arisen and events similar to Auschwitz have occurred in Rwanda, the Balkans, and Cambodia in recent years. There is a nearly unanimous global consensus that the crimes committed in these situations are evil. Even the most secular person would probably be willing to call these infamous behaviors *sin* and to condemn them in the strongest possible terms.

We're also quite willing to label as evil the random killing of school children by their classmates and murder in the workplace by disgruntled employees. I wish I could tell you that the Columbine High School killing spree in Colorado and Mark Barton's murder of his wife and children and nine people at two brokerage firms in Atlanta, Georgia are the most recent examples. Unfortunately, by the time you read these words, these events will almost certainly be overshadowed by others that are even worse.

Yet one of the oddities of human nature is that under certain circumstances, particularly during severe national or international crises, we humans will approve of actions that in more normal times we would absolutely reject. And that, I believe, is what will happen someday in our world. The evil that our society condemns so unhesitatingly today *it will one day approve*.

That's a strong statement, but I believe it because it's in the Bible.

Introduction to the crisis: Revelation 12:17

The situation I'm referring to is predicted in the Apocalypse, more commonly known as the biblical book of Revelation. As you may know, much of Revelation is a description of earth's final events just before the second coming of Christ, and the religious intolerance I'm talking about will occur at that time. The concluding verse in chapter 12 says:

> The dragon was enraged at the woman and went off to make war against the rest of her offspring.[2]

The author of Revelation is obviously using symbolic language here, and I'll explain the symbols in a moment. But we don't need a precise identification of the symbols in order to recognize that this short verse describes a bitter conflict. One party is out to destroy another. That's what war means. War prompted by bitter racial hatred led to the genocide in Rwanda and Cambodia and the "ethnic cleansing" in the former Yugoslavia. And when we look at the full picture in Revelation 13—which we'll do shortly—we discover that genocide, or perhaps "religious cleansing," is precisely the dragon's objective in his battle against the woman. To be sure you don't miss the point, I will state it in boldface letters:

Revelation predicts the rise of a horribly evil power in our world— one that today's United Nations would condemn in the strongest

**possible terms and intervene mili-
tarily to protect innocent human life
from it. This evil power will attempt
to stamp out all people who refuse
to go along with its religious agenda.
And most people in the world will
agree with what it is doing!**

That's the global spiritual crisis we're discussing in this chapter.

The question is, Who are the parties in this
conflict? Revelation identifies them as a dragon
and a woman. So who is this dragon, and who is
this woman?

Revelation itself answers the question about the
dragon. It calls the dragon "that ancient serpent
called the devil, or Satan."[3] And throughout the
Bible—both Old and New Testaments—a woman
is a symbol of God's people. In the Old Testament
God's people were the Jewish nation, and in the
New Testament they are the Christian church.

Revelation introduces us to this woman in
chapter 12:1, and at that point she's pregnant and
about to deliver a son. Revelation says that the
dragon "stood in front of the woman . . . so that
he might devour her child the moment it was
born."[4] That's an obvious reference to Herod's
command—inspired by Satan—to destroy the
Christ child by killing all the baby boys in
Bethlehem two years old and under.[5]

Revelation then says that "the woman fled into

the desert to a place prepared for her by God, where she might be taken care of for 1,260 days."[6] For several hundred years, Protestant students of prophecy have understood this to be a reference to the underground church of the Middle Ages that was so relentlessly persecuted by the Inquisition. However, when Revelation 12:17 describes the war between the dragon and the rest of the woman's offspring, it isn't talking about Satan's attack on Christ and Christians at the beginning of the Christian era nor during the Medieval period. This verse is introducing us to Satan's attack on God's people at the very end of time, shortly before the return of Jesus to our planet. Chapter 13 gives us the details.

The spiritual crisis in Revelation 13

Revelation 13 describes a terrible crisis that will come upon our planet shortly before the second coming of Christ—the war between the dragon and the woman that we've just been talking about. If you aren't familiar with chapter 13, I recommend that you pick up a Bible and read it now.

Revelation 13 begins by introducing us to a ferocious beast that "had ten horns and seven heads, with ten crowns on his horns, and on each head a blasphemous name."[7] And here's our first clue that this battle will be spiritual: The beast has blasphemous names written on each of its heads—an obvious suggestion that it's an enemy of God and that it will be an ally of Satan in his war against God's people.

But there's a much more important clue that the battle will be spiritual. Revelation goes on to say that "men worshiped . . . the beast."[8] Worship is a very spiritual act, as we all know, and verse 8 tells us that *the whole world* will worship this beast except for a very few whose names are written in the Lamb's book of life. The Lamb is a symbol of Christ, so the fact that Christ's followers refuse to participate in this worship means that it is a false form of worship.

But so what if most of the world worships this beast, and so what if God's people refuse to participate? Don't we live in a world that pretty much grants people the freedom to worship as they please? Isn't religious freedom written into the constitution of just about every country in the Western world? Isn't it a part of the United Nations charter? The mere fact that most people choose to worship one way and a few people worship another way doesn't mean they're fighting over it. Where's the battle?

Verse 7 introduces us to that:

> He [the beast] was given power to make war against the saints and to conquer them. And he was given authority over every tribe, people, language and nation.

This verse tells us several important things.

First, it specifically says that the beast will "make war against the saints"—that is, God's people. This is the dragon's war against the woman that we read about in chapter 12:17, except that the war will actually be carried out by Satan's agent, the beast with seven heads. And the beast will obviously prevail, at least for a time, because Revelation says it will *conquer* the saints.

Not only that, this beast will have global political power, because it will have authority "over every tribe, people, language and nation." So whatever the constitutions in today's Western countries may say about religious liberty, and whatever the United Nations may say about freedom of worship, a day is coming when a religious power that opposes these principles will control every nation on earth.

We're accustomed to religion dominating the political systems in certain Muslim countries—but the whole world? Strange as it may seem in our Western world, which is relatively free of religious oppression, that's what Revelation predicts. Not only that, the specific wording of verse 7 makes it clear that *the world as a whole will want it that way.* Notice: The beast "was *given* authority over every tribe, people, language and nation"; it "was *given* power to make war against the saints." This beast won't just reach out and grab political power on its own. The world will hand it over! The beast's war against God's people won't be just at its own initiative. The world will demand that it shut them up. This truly will be a global spiritual conflict. And it will be extremely intense. Just how intense, we discover in the last half of Revelation 13, where we meet another very strange beast—and an even more ominous one!

The second beast of Revelation 13

The first part of Revelation 13 describes the beast with seven heads and ten horns that we just read about. This beast arises out of the sea. Verse 11 describes a second beast that arises out of the earth. Revelation says that this land beast has two horns like a lamb, but it speaks like a dragon. Its two lamb-like horns suggest that it will be a Christian entity, but the fact that it speaks like a dragon means that it will actually be an agent of Satan. This land beast will deceive the entire world through certain miraculous signs, and verse 14 says it will order the world to set up an image to the sea beast. Now here's the clincher:

> He [the land beast] was given power to give breath to the image of the first beast, so that it could speak *and cause all who refused to worship the image to be killed.*[9]

Those who refuse to worship in the politically correct manner will be threatened with death! In fact, some probably *will* be put to death. And this enforced religion will be global, because "the inhabitants of the earth"[10] will set it up. The only way to escape the land beast's wrath will be to accept the mark of the sea beast. Anyone who refuses this mark will be forbidden to carry out even the simplest business transaction—buying and selling. And the underlying issue will be spiritual.

This is the evil that is coming to our world. This is the global spiritual crisis that we are destined to confront in the very near future.

That's incredible! you say. Something like that surely would be the height of evil—but in our Western culture, which for hundreds of years has placed such a premium on freedom of religion?

I agree that the scenario presented in Revelation 13 sounds almost impossible in today's world. I wouldn't believe it myself were it not that the Bible predicts it. But how could an evil spiritual crisis of that intensity ever embrace our whole planet?

Quite simply, actually. I believe it will be precipitated by the global natural disasters that the Bible also predicts, which we learned about in the previous chapter. Now I must be honest and tell you that nowhere does Revelation 13 actually link the global natural disasters with the global spiritual crisis. But the Bible *does* tell us that both the global natural disasters and the global spiritual crisis will occur at the same time—in the weeks and months immediately preceding Christ's second coming. And I propose that the global spiritual crisis predicted in Revelation 13 will be humanity's response to the global physical crisis that I described in the previous chapter. For as I pointed out earlier in this chapter, during a severe national or international crisis, we human beings will approve of what, in more normal times, we would absolutely reject.

Before concluding this chapter, I would like to explain to you what I believe will *really* be going on when this crisis erupts.

Several thousand years ago, Satan, who at the time was an angel in heaven, challenged God's sovereignty over the universe. Eventually his rebellion broke out into the open, and he and his sympathizers were cast out of heaven and down to the earth. For thousands of years now our planet has been the theater in which Satan has waged his war against God's government. Naturally, a major focus of his attack has been those people—the Bible calls them saints—who retain their loyalty to God. It is not surprising, then, that at the very end of time, when the battle between God and Satan reaches its most white-hot intensity, Satan's attack against God's people will be more severe than at any other time in the history of the world.

When that time comes, it will be extremely important that you and I understand what's going on. And if it's true that the greatest spiritual crisis in the history of the world lies just ahead of us, the most important issue for you and me today is how to be spiritually prepared for what's coming.

Which is what the rest of this book is about.

---

[1]Associated Press article, "'Hitler's Niece' looks at Fuhrer's first love," The Idaho Statesman, August 29, 1999, 1E.

[2]Revelation 12:17.

[3]Revelation 12:9.

[4]Verses 1-5.

[5]Matthew 1:16.

[6]Revelation 12:6.

[7]Revelation 13:1.

[8]Verse 4.

[9]Verse 15, italics supplied.

[10]Verse 14.

Spirituality

Pick your disaster: Hurricane, tornado, earthquake, volcano, or some terrorist blowing up a government building. Regardless of when or where it happens, each of these disasters is a crisis that creates a unique bond among the people who experience it.

Take hurricane Floyd, for example, which sent flood waters washing over North Carolina in September 1999. For the rest of their lives, the people who went through that disaster will have a camaraderie that they share with no one else. They may tell stories about it to others, but they can reminisce about it only with those who went through the experience with them.

The same thing will be true of the coming global crisis. Those of us who pass through that time will have an experience that we can *tell* others about, but we will find the most meaning in talking about it with those who went through the crisis with us.

There's a unique collective experience shared by everyone who passes through a traumatic event together. But now think of this: *There's also a sense in which each individual experiences the trauma alone.*

One of the things that draws husbands and wives closer together as the years go by is the crises they pass through together. Yet as close as they are to each other, even husbands and wives must experience every one of these shared crises on their own. Each has to find his or her own answers to the spiritual questions these crises raise. I gave my wife Lois comfort and support through her recovery from the pit bull attack. We talked about the spiritual issues, and I shared my thoughts with her, but she had to find her own answers.

That's also how it will be during earth's final crisis. While you and I will pass through that time with many other people, in a very real sense we will experience it as though we were the only human beings alive. Nobody else will be able to live our spirituality for us. No one else will be able to make our choices for us. Regardless of the number of people around us—even if they are believers—we will have to make those spiritual choices ourselves.

This also means that no one else can *prepare* us for the final crisis. You can't prepare me, and I can't prepare you. Each of us must make our own spiritual preparation.

And that's what the rest of this book is about. I hope the plan for spiritual growth and maturity that I discuss in the next few chapters will also help you to pass through the smaller crises in your life between now and then. For as I pointed out in a previous chapter, if we handle them properly, each small crisis prepares us a little better for the next one.

So let's get started.

What is spirituality?

If it's going to take a spiritual experience to make it through the coming global crisis without falling apart, then it's important that we understand spirituality. I will begin by proposing that every human being is profoundly spiritual.

"But I'm not religious!" you may protest.

Thanks for telling me, but religion and spirituality are actually two quite different things. Not all people are religious, but all people are spiritual. You and I can no more escape being spiritual than we can escape being physical. Spirituality is as much a part of our nature as our reason and our emotions. It's not just doctors, lawyers, and scientists who are rational. To be human is to be rational, because our brains are wired that way. It's not just the artists, musicians, and poets among us who are emotional. We're all emotional, because our brains are wired that way.

In the same way, I propose that the brains of all human beings are wired to be spiritual.

Spirituality has to do with our human capacity to appreciate music, art, and the beauty of nature. The rapture you and I experience when listening to a haunting melody, the awe we sense when gazing at a beautiful sunset, or the warm glow that comes over us when we cuddle a baby in our arms—each of these is a spiritual experience.

Spirituality has to do with our ability to distinguish between good and evil. Honesty is a spiritual issue. So is dishonesty. When I am honest with you I'm exercising my spirituality, but I'm also exercising the spiritual part of my nature when I'm dishonest. Mercy and justice are spiritual issues. When I treat you kindly, I'm exercising the spiritual part of my nature, but so is the person who treats you unkindly. One of us is being spiritual in a positive sense, the other in a negative sense. Does it seem strange to you that I should speak of dishonesty and cruelty as spiritual issues? The Bible talks about "spiritual forces of evil in the heavenly realms."[1]

Spirituality has to do with our priorities, the things we value. Which is more important to you, things or relationships? Your job or your family? Money or people? Given the option of spending ten dollars for something you want or something your child wants, which will you choose—and most important, Why? There may be a valid reason for spending money on your choice rather than your child's. Spirituality has to do with *why* you made that choice. Was it because you wanted what *you* wanted or because you knew that what your child wanted in this instance truly would not be in his or her best interest? And were you honest with yourself in that decision or just rationalizing to get your way? Our answers to questions such as these reveal our true spirituality.

In a sense, spirituality is the same thing as character. Character is what you and I are like on the inside. It's how we respond to ethical situations. What do you do, for example, when you have a chance to cheat on the IRS and get away with it? If you are an honest person at heart, you will be honest with the IRS even though it means disadvantaging yourself. A dishonest person will opt for the personal advantage. Your character— the kind of person you are on the inside—will determine your response. But as we have already noted, honesty and dishonesty are also spiritual issues. They are the positive and negative sides of spirituality. That's why spirituality is very similar to character. In fact, Webster's dictionary defines spirituality as "spiritual character, quality or nature."[2]

Spirituality and the coming global crisis

So what kind of spiritual challenges are we likely to face during the coming global crisis?

During World War II, most Christians, both Protestant and Catholic, refused to oppose the genocide that was being perpetrated against the Jews by the Nazi regime. Perhaps some Christians were ignorant of what Hitler and his thugs were doing, but many knew enough that they should have taken a stand for what was right. The reason they didn't was fear. Very few Christians in Germany during World War II had the courage to speak out against what they knew was going on.

That's a spiritual issue.

It takes a tough character and a profound spirituality to recognize evil and speak out against it in the face of death. But the Christians in Germany seem to have been swept up right along with everyone else in the popular enthusiasm for Hitler. Some of them even approved of what he was doing! And what happened on a national scale in Germany during World War II will be repeated on a global scale during the final crisis. In the previous chapter we learned that the world as a whole will *give* authority to the beast powers that are persecuting God's people. Most people will *approve* of the religious cleansing that Revelation describes.

So the question for you and me, if we are alive during that time, is whether we will take our stand for what is right, or whether we will take the easy, popular way out, and join the side of evil. And just as this choice was spiritual in Germany during World War II, so it will be during earth's final crisis. The question is, *Will you and I have the spirituality, the strength of character, to stand for the right though the heavens fall?*

Spirituality

I can assure you of one thing: We must develop this spiritual strength of character *before* the crisis begins. If we don't have it ahead of time, it will be too late to develop it once the crisis is underway.

The theme of this book is very simple: A crisis is both a test of our present spirituality and a springboard into a deeper spirituality. We can easily learn from a minor crisis without too much disruption in our life, but a major crisis can have catastrophic consequences—such as losing our health, our financial security, or our family. The crisis will provide us an opportunity for further growth—but this growth will come too late to be of any use in dealing with the present situation.

I propose that the coming global crisis will be so catastrophic that if you and I aren't making the necessary spiritual preparation now, it will be too late to make the preparation when the crisis hits. The question is, What can you and I do today and tomorrow and the next day to prepare for this crisis?

Several things, actually. Keep reading.

---

[1]Ephesians 6:12.
[2]*Webster's New World Dictionary*, Second College Edition (New York: Simon and Schuster, 1982).

5

Insight

Several years ago I received a booklet in the mail advertising a course on commodity trading. The booklet was definitely in the category of junk mail, which I typically throw away without even opening. However, I recognized this course as one that a friend had recommended a couple of years earlier. For a number of years I'd been mildly curious about trading in stocks and commodities, so I decided to risk the $200 for the course.

I was actually quite pleased with what I learned, and within a few weeks I was paper trading in commodities. Paper trading is a learning exercise in which one watches the charts for potentially profitable moves and keeps records as though it were real trading. My paper trading went quite well, so I signed up with a broker and began trading with money. One of the principles of trading in stocks or commodities is to risk no more than you can afford to lose, so I decided ahead of time the amount I was willing to risk and determined not to exceed that in case I lost more than I earned.

Insight

I soon learned that trading with real money is quite different from trading on paper. While I made several profitable trades, the overall trend was negative, and within about three months I had lost all of my risk money.

The problem, however, was not that the markets acted differently when I began trading with real money. The markets didn't say, "Ah ha! This guy has started trading real money. Let's reach out and bite him!" The difference between paper trading and money trading was with me, not the markets. I was emotionally out of control. Here are some of my reactions to trading with money.

- I became anxious and very nervous.
- Commodities were on my mind all the time, and trading caused me to neglect important areas of my personal life.
- I obsessed so much about commodities that I couldn't sleep at night. Several nights I never slept at all, and those nights when I did sleep I usually had a hard time dropping off to sleep. I'd also wake up at 3:00 or 4:00 in the morning and couldn't go back to sleep.
- My emotions were on a roller coaster ride. I was overly elated when I made money and deeply depressed when I lost money.
- I made spur-of-the-moment decisions instead of studying the charts and reflecting carefully before making an investment.

- I was vaguely aware of being out of control, but I was so excited about trading that I pushed the thought to the back of my mind.
- I had told very few people what I was doing, but I moaned loud and long about my terrible misfortune to those few.

I'll never forget the day I lost the last bit of my risk money. I was wired, a nervous wreck, absolutely incapable of concentrating on anything else. I immediately quit trading real money, but it took me several days to settle down emotionally to the point where I could sleep well at night.

In the weeks that followed I spent a good bit of time reflecting on what had happened, especially my emotional frame of mind. Fortunately, for the previous several years I had been fairly diligent in following what is popularly known as a "recovery program." I had read a lot of recovery literature, attended many Twelve-Step meetings, and made a serious effort to implement the Twelve Steps to recover from my addictions. All of this had taught me a lot about the nature of addiction and its symptoms. And I realized that *my response to commodity trading was a classic case study in addictive behavior*. In fact, I came to the sobering conclusion that I was an excellent candidate for becoming a full-blown gambling addict! Following are the symptoms of addiction that I exhibited during my introduction to commodity trading:

- Obsession about commodities, which was evident in my continual thinking about commodities during the day and my inability to sleep at night.
- Compulsive behavior, which was evident in the frenzied, impulsive investments I made without consulting the charts and the rules for wise investing.
- Fear and anxiety, which were the underlying cause of my obsessive-compulsive behavior.
- Denial of what was really going on in my life, which was evident in my awareness of my out-of-control behavior, but pushing it to the back of my mind.
- Neglect of other important personal responsibilities. In recovery terms, my life had become unmanageable.
- Moaning and groaning to others about my misery, which in recovery circles is called "martyring."
- I hit bottom. I ran out of risk money.

Why have I told you this story, which is obviously quite personal and not very flattering? Because it illustrates so well the point of this chapter: *We all have spiritual defects, but we can't correct what we aren't aware of.*

Thoughts, feelings, and behavior

In spite of the fact that unwise commodity trading cost me a significant amount of money, that wasn't my basic problem. The basic problem was spiritual. Spirituality has to do with our thoughts and feelings—what you and I are like on the inside.[1] And for the most part our thoughts and feelings determine our behavior—how we respond to what happens to us.

For example, what do you do when you're running late to an important appointment? You step on the gas (behavior). Why? Because you *know* you're late (thoughts), and you're *afraid* of missing the appointment (feelings). But if you see a police car up ahead you'll apply the brake (behavior), because you *know* the police car represents the law (thoughts), and you're *afraid* the officer will ticket you for speeding (feelings).

We can say, then, that our spirituality—our thoughts and feelings—determines our behavior. And if we notice that our behavior is flawed, we can know that something isn't quite right on the inside. For example, if you frequently catch yourself losing your temper (behavior), you can be fairly certain that something is wrong with the way you *think* and *feel* about life.

Now think back for a moment on my behavior with commodities. I was totally out of control. My behavior was very flawed. And if flawed behavior is a symptom of a flawed spirituality, then my out-of-control behavior with commodities was a clear indication that *I had a major spiritual defect*. In fact, this defect was so serious that had I failed to correct it I would eventually have gone bankrupt!

Insight

Most of us, when confronted with flawed behavior, focus our attention on changing the behavior. But this usually works only for a short time. Unless we change the spiritual defect on the inside, we are doomed to continue the flawed behavior on the outside. This principle is so important that I'm going to repeat it in boldface letters:

**Unless we change the spiritual defect on the inside,
we are doomed to continue the flawed behavior on the outside.**

Let's apply this principle to my experience with commodities. My thoughts about commodities were flawed. I had very unrealistic expectations of what would happen when I called my broker and made a contract. I was also tense and anxious—powerful emotions that were also very flawed. There's no way I was going to relate properly to commodities without a major change in my thoughts and feelings. Or, to say it the way we're discussing it here, there was no way I could relate properly to commodities without correcting these defects in my spirituality.

Crisis and denial

There was one huge problem, though. Think back to what I said about myself during the time I was running around chasing all those commodities: "I was vaguely aware of being out of control, but I was so excited about trading that *I pushed the thought to the back of my mind."*

That's denial, which is one of the major symptoms of addiction.

In order to correct a spiritual defect, we have to break out of our denial about it. We have to reach the point that we're willing to admit we have a problem. But how can we do that when we're up to our eyeballs in denial? That's where a crisis comes in so handy! Because *a crisis will expose our spiritual defects.* We don't like being in a state of crisis, of course, but that's beside the point. If a crisis will expose our spiritual defects, then it serves a very useful purpose.

Some of the crises that life throws our way are random events over which we have no control, and we are in no way to blame for them. You don't blame yourself when a drunk runs a stop sign and smashes into your car, when a tornado destroys your home, or when a plane crash kills a loved one.

However, a great many of the crises we deal with in life are a result of our own mistakes. We create these crises by the bad decisions we make. And so often these bad decisions are a result of our out-of-control emotions. We may be vaguely aware of the problem, but *we enjoy whatever it is that's heading us toward trouble*—as I did with my out-of-control trading—so we push the warning aside (denial) and continue in our self-destructive behavior. We persist in the denial because we enjoy what we're doing, and because the consequences of each individual bad decision seem quite insignificant. Not until these smaller decisions have accumulated to the point that we hit bottom and can't keep going any further do we realize that we really *do* have a problem. Now, regardless of how much we may *enjoy* the particular behavior, we are forced to admit that it's gotten us into deep trouble.

Crises come in degrees, of course. They aren't all devastating. They don't all land us in the hospital, the divorce court, or the morgue. Some are just irritants. These smaller, earlier crises are important, though, as warning signals of danger ahead. For example:

- Your midnight drinking party leaves you with such a splitting headache that you call in sick the next morning—for the third time in two weeks.
- You find yourself juggling the finances each month to keep the utilities, the phone bill, and the mortgage paid up—and all the credit cards.
- Your spouse slept in the spare bedroom the night after your most recent fight.
- You catch yourself increasingly short of breath, and your doctor advises you to quit smoking.

Each of these so-called "minor crises" is a flag waving in your face or mine, urging us to open our eyes and pay attention to what is actually a very serious problem. And each of us is infected with these spiritual defects that get us into trouble. If we don't correct the problem when we encounter the first crisis, the next one will probably be worse. If the alcoholic doesn't heed the first warning signal, somewhere down the line he's likely to lose his job. The credit card junkie who ignores the earlier warning signals will eventually go bankrupt, the abusive spouse may find himself or herself in the divorce court, and the smoker is in danger of coming down with a full-blown case of cancer or emphysema.

The key to breaking out of denial, then, is to pay attention to the crises in your life, and the earlier the better. The next time something really bad happens to you, instead of blaming someone else for the problem, ask yourself if the situation is a result of your own misjudgment or of some flaw in *you*.

I have good news for you: The more you do this, the easier it will get. Let's go back to my experience with commodities. Even though I was in denial over my out-of-control behavior for several weeks, when I ran out of risk money *I did stop*. Had I been a full-blown addict I'd have kept going and risked money I couldn't afford to lose. But because I had been active in a program of recovery from other addictions for several years, I recognized the potential new addiction when it popped up in my life, and I knew what to do about it. Fifteen years earlier I would have had a much harder time recognizing and dealing with the problem.

This illustrates again the major theme of this book: that a crisis is both a test of our present spirituality and an opportunity to further develop our spirituality. My crisis with commodities was a test of what I had learned over the previous several years, and it showed that I had indeed developed some healthy spiritual traits. But it also was clear evidence that I still had a way to go in this particular area, and in doing so it opened up an opportunity for continued spiritual growth that I had been totally ignorant of up to that point.

This explains a text in the Bible that sounds very strange the first time you read it: "Consider it pure joy, my brothers, whenever you face trials [crises] of many kinds, because you know that the testing of your faith develops perseverance."[2]

That *is* strange, isn't it? How can anyone *rejoice* over trials? How can anyone feel *thankful* for trouble? I don't think God expects us to be happy about the crises in our lives. He wants us to rejoice over the opportunity they provide for spiritual growth.

Breaking out of our denial

Every now and then I see a serious problem in someone else's life, yet that person is totally oblivious to the situation. Even when I bring the subject up to this person, he or she will often say, "Oh, no, that's not a problem for me at all."

That's denial, and I'm sure you've seen people like that too.

Now here's the tough question: Has it ever occurred to you that you might suffer from the same malady?

Regardless of what you *think* the answer is, let me tell you what I know it is for me and what I'm quite sure it is for you: Yes. *This is a universal human problem.*

Why are we so loathe to believe the truth about ourselves, even when the evidence is clearly in front of us? I'd like to suggest two reasons.

We enjoy our vices. The first reason is that we like our sins. Never mind that these vices are destroying us. They feel good, and we want to hang on to them. Even when we know they're destroying us, we return to them time and again the way a dog licks up its vomit. We fool ourselves into believing that we're in control. We think we can handle our cherished vice very well thank you, and we'll appreciate all those who are trying to point out the problem to bug out of our life.

Pride. The second reason why we humans are so loath to admit our shortcomings is pride. Now it's OK to have a healthy self-esteem. Jesus said that we should love our neighbor *as we love ourselves.*[3] But self-esteem, like happiness, does not come by looking for it. The search for self-esteem easily becomes an obsession that destroys the very peace of mind that it's trying to find.

Insight

And that's precisely where pride comes in. Pride is a distorted effort to preserve our self-esteem. A person with genuine self-esteem feels reasonably comfortable looking at his or her weaknesses as well as strengths. Pride is a denial of the truth about our shortcomings so that we can "look good" to ourselves. Unfortunately, those who do that will never gain genuine self-esteem, because they can never make themselves truly worthwhile as long as they refuse to deal with those things that make them less than worthwhile.

So how can we break out of this denial?

The answer to that question is simple. We can't do it on our own. This is especially true for those attitudes and habits that are deeply ingrained within our psyches. For these issues we need an external source of help that is greater than we are. I don't care whether you call this external source of help "God,"[4] "Higher Power," or some other name. You and I are powerless to change our own inner nature. In order to deal effectively with these problems of the spirit, we must have outside help.

So the first step in dealing with a crisis is to break out of denial and acknowledge our character defects. And for that we need God's help. Fortunately, it's easy to get His help. All we have to do is say this prayer:

God, show me the defects in my life, and make me willing to accept what I see.

THE COMING GLOBAL CRISIS

I've prayed this prayer many times in the last few years, and I can tell you that it works. The results aren't always fun. God is wise enough to know that one of the ways we human beings are most likely to face up to our defects is through a crisis. So the next time you're in the middle of a crisis, remind yourself of that prayer and look for the lesson in the crisis.

Let's summarize in one sentence what we've discussed in this chapter: In order to experience spiritual growth, we must first recognize the defects in our characters that need correcting.

However, recognizing a defect is only the first step in getting rid of it. There are a number of other things we can do to actually *overcome* our spiritual problems.

So let's get into it.

---

[1]A close relationship exists between character and spirituality. In many ways they are the same thing. Character is also our thoughts and feelings—what we are like on the inside. And character also determines behavior. For our purpose in this book these terms are interchangeable. In other books I have written I have used the word *character*. However, since we began with the word *spirituality* in this book, I am continuing it in this chapter.

[2]James 1:2, 3.

[3]Matthew 22:39.

[4]Most people choose, as I do, to call this outside source of help *God*. Even many atheists have recognized, when they bottomed out, that there was insufficient power within themselves to deal with their overpowering emotions. They needed outside help.

CHAPTER 6

Grace

I'm not sure why Hollywood hasn't picked up on the story. It has all the makings of the kind of sex-and-romance movie that rakes in the big bucks at the box office. I would have thought that Paramount or Universal Studios would surely have turned it into a film long ago—or perhaps Dreamworks, since they're into Bible stories these days.

It began on what was probably a hot summer afternoon in old Jerusalem. A rather large crowd had gathered in the temple courtyard to hear Jesus teach. In my mind, I picture Him holding a child on His lap as He answers the people's questions. Suddenly a woman's scream pierces the air, followed by the shouts of angry male voices. The disturbance seems to be coming from the street outside the temple courtyard and, of course, the people turn to see what's going on.

A moment later a dozen or so men burst into the courtyard, half dragging, half pushing a woman toward Jesus. They throw her face down in the center of the crowd. Their hostility is thick enough to breathe, but from the dark glances they cast from Him to her and back at Him it's hard to tell who they're more angry at.

The woman's fingers claw the pavement. Her body shakes, and she weeps quietly. Her tears form dark spots in the dust. But the men don't give her much time for weeping. They jerk her to her feet and shove her toward Jesus. She stumbles forward, her head bowed, a hand over her face. Then she starts sinking to the ground again. A tall man, who appears to be the spokesman for the group, grabs her arm. "Now you stand!" he orders. "And I want you to look at *Him!*" He spits out the word *Him*.

"But Eliab, why?" the woman pleads. "You're the one who promised me . . ."

Eliab gives her another shove, then steps forward and addresses Jesus. "Sir," he sneers, "this woman—Johanna is her name—was caught in the very act of adultery."[1] He pauses and looks around at the crowd, and a faint smile crosses his face as he hears their murmur of astonishment. Then fixing his eyes on Jesus he continues: "In the Law Moses commanded us to stone such women. What do You say?"

Jesus looks from one of the men to the other without saying a word. Two or three of them begin to fidget, but Jesus just stands with His hands at His side.

Finally, Eliab speaks again. "Well?"

Grace

Jesus kneels and starts writing with His finger in a dusty spot on the pavement. Irritated at His apparent indifference, Eliab demands, "What's Your verdict?"

Jesus keeps on writing.

Eliab leans toward Jesus, and His voice is louder: "I said, what's *Your* verdict?"

Jesus puts a hand on one knee and rises slowly to His feet. He fixes His gaze on one, then another of the men surrounding Him. At last, gesturing toward Johanna, who by now has fallen back on the pavement and is weeping again, He says, "Gentlemen, the one among you who is without sin will please cast the first stone." Then He kneels and resumes writing in the dust.

Curious now, one of the men steps toward Jesus and looks down at the pavement where He's writing. He leans over and turns his head to see better. Suddenly he gasps, and without saying a word he hurries away. Jesus brushes the dust to erase the words, then starts writing again. Eliab peers over Jesus' shoulder, then he too gasps and leaves. The scene is repeated till not one man remains of those who had dragged Johanna into Jesus' presence.

When all have left, Jesus stands and turns toward Johanna. She's curled up face down on the pavement. Her choking sobs come from deep within her throat, and her body heaves as she weeps, not daring to look up for shame over the public exposure of her deed and terror over her imminent fate. Jesus steps over and rests a hand on her shoulder. "Woman," He says gently, but she's too deeply troubled to even be aware of His presence. He pauses a moment, then repeats, "Woman," and this time He gives her shoulder a light shake. "Woman, where are your accusers?" Jesus leaves His hand on her shoulder as He awaits her reply.

Johanna's weeping subsides slowly, but at last she rises on one elbow, and for a moment she looks around as though she's in a daze. Suddenly she jerks to a sitting position, and one by one she gazes at the crowd surrounding her. She studies each face. At last she turns back to Jesus, and awe is in her voice when she speaks. "They're all gone," she whispers. "There are no accusers."

Jesus takes her hand and raises it slightly. She remains sitting quietly for a moment, then slowly rises to her feet. "Neither do I accuse you," He says. He leans toward her just slightly and looks into her eyes with a warm smile.

She searches His face, as if trying to understand, as though what He just said doesn't make any sense. But slowly, as His smile and His words penetrate her mind, a light replaces the pain in her eyes. She brushes a strand of hair from her face and smiles back at Him.

Jesus reaches out with His right hand and touches her arm. "Now go home," He says softly, "and see to it that you don't sin any more."

Grace

I wish I could tell you what happened next, but that's as far as the Bible carries the story. Of one thing I'm reasonably certain, though. I don't think Johanna just dashed off with a quick "Thanks! See ya 'round." In my mind, I picture her throwing her arms around Jesus' neck, resting her head on His shoulder, and shaking as she sobs. Or she falls to her knees and sobs as she clutches His feet. Perhaps in their culture that would have been more acceptable.

So what are we to make of this story? At the very least, we can say that Johanna faced a horrible crisis, the likes of which I'm sure each of us hopes never to confront. However, if we'll reflect on it carefully, Johanna's story has some good lessons that can help us as we cope with the crises that come our way from day to day. I'd like to examine some of those lessons in the next few pages, especially Johanna's self-esteem and how Jesus related to her self-esteem.

Johanna's self-esteem

Of all the issues we deal with, one of the most spiritual is our view of ourselves—whether we have high or low self-esteem. People with low self-esteem are more likely to be in conflict with others. Young people with low self-esteem are more likely than those with high self-esteem to use alcohol and other drugs and engage in premarital sex. While it would be an oversimplification to say that all evil arises out of low self-esteem, that is a major contributing factor to evil behavior, because people with low self-esteem tend to be so focused on themselves that they are unable to relate to others with respect and proper regard.

It's important to understand that for the most part we do not create our own self-esteem. We tend to value ourselves the way we believe other people value us. So much of our self-esteem comes from our relationships with others. If those around us express appreciation for us, we are more likely to feel good about ourselves. On the other hand, if the people we deal with on a daily basis put us down, our self-esteem is likely to be quite low. Many of the teenage boys who shot up their classmates and teachers in the past few years had very low self-esteem, because they were the objects of ridicule by the more popular students in their schools.

Unfortunately, low self-esteem causes us to make foolish mistakes. Often our intention is to feel better about ourselves, but the decisions backfire on us, and we end up feeling worse than before. That's why we tend to bring our crises upon ourselves. And for those of us who are caught up in this spiral, until we can solve the problem of our low self-esteem and begin thinking straight, our bad choices will keep getting us into one crisis after another, each one worse than the one before, until we finally hit bottom.

Let's go back now to Johanna. What was going on in her mind and emotions as she lay weeping on the pavement in front of Jesus and that crowd of people? Publicly humiliated and condemned of one of the most abhorrent of all sins in that culture, her sense of self-worth must have been somewhere down in the bottom of a deep, dark pit.

For those of us who believe in God, the most important source of our self-esteem is in what He thinks of us—or, more correctly, what we *believe* He thinks of us. Because Johanna lived in a culture that believed in God, it's safe to assume that she also believed in God. Surely, by the time the men who brought her to Jesus had finished with their accusations, any sense of self-worth that she may have had in her relationship with God was totally destroyed. If she believed in heaven and hell, she must have felt absolutely convinced that God was about to send her straight to the hot place. For how could a holy and righteous God ever accept her after what she had just done! She was a wicked, evil woman, and she deserved God's utter wrath. Every last bit of it! She was probably thinking, "I'm the scum of the earth, and God abhors me!"

What a horrible self-image!

Jesus and Johanna
Coming back now to Jesus, I'd like to propose an interesting thought: that the men who brought her to Him did not cast a total stranger

at His feet. I think He was already acquainted with her. I say this because of the way He treated her. Ask yourself, for example, how Jesus would have treated a hardened prostitute who had no intention of abandoning her way of life, who perhaps was even proud of her profession. While He would not have been rude to such a woman, I think His words to her would have been quite different.

The idea that Jesus and Johanna were already acquainted suggests some interesting—and I think significant—conclusions.

If there's one thing Jesus enjoyed doing more than anything else, it was mentoring people spiritually. That was the great passion of His life. And He mentored women as well as men. The Bible tells us that Mary, the sister of Lazarus and Martha, sat at His feet and listened with rapt attention to His words.[2] On another occasion, shortly before His death, a woman whom He had mentored wept as she bathed His feet with an expensive perfume.[3] Some Bible students have even suggested that the woman I've called Johanna was the same woman in the other two situations. If this is true, then Johanna was *very* well acquainted with Jesus at the time she lay weeping on the pavement, accused of adultery.

Now consider with me another significant possibility in this story about Johanna. I suspect the truth in her situation goes beyond the outward appearance of the one adulterous act the

Bible tells us about. Sex is a powerful emotion in both sexes, and it's one to which we easily become addicted. Indeed, recovering sexual addicts who have also struggled with alcohol and other drugs quite consistently tell us that they found the drugs much easier to deal with. Even more common than sexual addiction in women is relationship addiction—the obsessive search for another human being to understand and accept them. Women often fall into sexual sin as a path to relationships. Was this Johanna's problem? The mere fact that she was caught in an adulterous relationship lends credence to that possibility.

Addicts have very low self-esteem, and their addictive behavior is the result of choices they made to feel good about themselves. Of course, as I pointed out earlier, these choices backfire, leaving addicts feeling worse about themselves each time, till at last they make the final destructive choice: They hit bottom. And at that point what little self-esteem they might have had left is totally shattered. Johanna ended up an object of loathing—publicly exposed as an adulteress and threatened with death by stoning. That's about as far down as a person can get in the self-esteem department.

Now let's come back to Jesus. If He was already acquainted with her and had been her spiritual mentor, and if she was struggling with a sexual or relationship addiction, then He almost certainly had tried to help her in this area of her life as well. If this is true, then the day her tears spilled onto the pavement in front of a crowd of onlookers was not the first time Johanna had wept in Jesus' presence over this issue. And if she'd felt ashamed before when she and Jesus talked about her addiction, now she must have felt absolutely awful. She'd made a mess of her life again, this time in public—in front of her Friend, her Mentor!

Then there's God. Johanna obviously didn't have time in the few moments she lay weeping on the pavement to run a major theological reflection on God and sin through her mind. Nevertheless, God was in the background of the whole situation. For starters, the men who dragged her into Jesus' presence accused her of breaking God's law. And Jesus, who up to that point had been her Friend and Mentor, was God's own representative. So if God's approval is the most important element in our self-esteem, then at that moment Johanna had absolutely no basis whatsoever to think of herself as anything but the scum of the earth.

Jesus' response to Johanna

We all struggle with the question, What does God think of me? And because we all have our moral failings, it's easy to believe, like Johanna, that God is angry with us, that He condemns us. That's why Jesus' treatment of Johanna comes to each of us as such marvelous good news! For after asking her where her accusers were, the very next words out of His mouth were, "Neither do I condemn you."

Now figure that one out! Here's a Man who claims to represent God, standing in front of a woman who has just violated God's commandment against adultery, and *He* says, "I don't condemn you"! Did God suddenly change His mind about His own law? Did He momentarily forget His law? Or did He perhaps decide to make an exception in this case?

The answer is none of the above. After all, Jesus did say to Johanna, " 'Go now and leave your life of sin.' "[4] So He acknowledged that what she had done was wrong. Then why did He say "Neither do I condemn you"? And the answer is . . .

Grace

Grace means that God accepts sinners right where they are, with all the dismal record of their past sins and the defects in their characters that will keep them sinning for a very long time.[5] Another name for that is *forgiveness*. Most religions in the world teach that God accepts good people and rejects bad people. But Christianity turns that idea around 180 degrees and says that God accepts bad people. There are two reasons for this. First and most important is that He loves us. He cares about us. And second, He wants to *help* us turn our lives around. In fact, He knows that He *has* to help us, because we are powerless to reform our lives on our own.

And He begins by forgiving all our past mistakes and accepting us right where we are. *That's how He heals our broken self-esteem.* God's acceptance of us, His forgiveness at the very start of our walk with Him, is the first step in His long process of healing our self-esteem so that we can gradually turn our life around and stop making those stupid mistakes[6] that keep getting us into one crisis after another.

I pointed out earlier that our self-esteem is based largely on what others think of us. That being true, one of the most important things we can do for others is give them our unconditional positive regard. Among other things, this means accepting them the way they are. We build people's self-esteem when we do this. And since our most important relationship is with God, the most healing thing that can happen to our self-esteem is to know that He accepts us unconditionally. That's what forgiveness is all about. That's what grace is all about.

And that's what Jesus did for Johanna. He accepted her right where she was. When He said, "Neither do I condemn you," He showed her unconditional positive regard. He forgave her. *He gave her back her self-esteem.*

Reflect for a moment on what that must have meant to Johanna right then. She's lying on the pavement, publicly humiliated in front of God's own representative because of her shameful deed. Her self-esteem is at the bottom of this deep, dark pit. And God's representative whispers in her ear, "I don't condemn you." What a relief that must have been! That's why I showed her weeping on His shoulder or at His feet.

And that's why Johanna's story is such good news to all of us. We've messed up our lives, bottomed out, disappointed our loved ones and ourselves—and God gives us back our self-esteem. He accepts us right where we are!

Justification

Let's get technical for a moment. The Bible has a theological term for what we've learned about God's grace. It's called *justification*. Before you panic over that long word, let me assure you that the definition is very simple, and it's very good news. To justify means to put one thing in a right relationship with something else. In the Bible's use of the word, justification means that we are put right with God. To put it in simpler language, He forgives us. He accepts us right where we are, from the best sinner (if there is such a thing) down to the worst.

That's grace.

Now think of this: If our self-esteem depends to a large extent on our relationship with God, then when we've been put right with God, we have the foundation for positive self-esteem.

THE COMING GLOBAL CRISIS

One of the most significant things about God's plan isn't just that He has a way to put us right with Himself; it's *how* He does it. All of the world's great religions, Christianity included, recognize the problem of evil and the importance of human beings living good moral lives. And, according to most of the world's religions, the way to gain God's favor is to live right. But as I pointed out a moment ago, Christianity turns that idea around 180 degrees. Christianity says that God accepts us right where we are, regardless of how sinful we may have been. To put it another way, *obedience is not a qualification for our acceptance by God.* He doesn't require us to reform our lives, or even make a tiny beginning at reforming our lives, before He will accept us and extend to us His unconditional positive regard.

Would you like the proof of that? Let me share with you a couple of verses from the Bible. Here's the first one:

> For we maintain that a man is justified by faith apart from observing the law.[7]

Notice that we are justified "apart from observing the law." To observe the law means to keep the Ten Commandments, or any of the other requirements in the Bible for that matter. The point is that God accepts us, He puts us right with Himself, regardless of how evil our lives have been up to that point. Now, if our self-esteem is to a great extent based on what *we* think *God* thinks of us, and if all along we've thought He condemned us because of our bad behavior, then the good news is that God doesn't consider our bad behavior when He decides to accept us. (This doesn't mean that God is indifferent to our bad behavior or that obedience doesn't count for anything with Him. I'll comment on that in a moment.)

The point is that when we come to Him, He takes us right where we are—bad behavior, flawed character, everything. He does it this way for a good reason. He knows that as long as we think of ourselves as the scum of the earth, we won't be able to make any progress toward the obedience and good behavior that's His ultimate ideal for us. That's why He accepts us right where we are, and then He helps us develop the good behavior.

Faith—the condition for acceptance by God

Earlier I spoke about two texts that affirm God's acceptance of us apart from our obedience of His requirements. We've looked at the first one. The second one puts it all in the context of grace:

It is by grace you have been saved, through faith—and this not from yourselves, it is the gift of God—not by works, so that no one can boast.[8]

Does this mean that there are no conditions to our acceptance by God? Of course not! Each of the two Bible texts I just quoted state the conditions clearly:

> "A man is justified *by faith* apart from observing the law."
> "It is by grace you have been saved, *through faith*, . . . not by works."

We are put right with God through *faith*. I'll go into much more detail about faith in a later chapter, but for now let me share with you briefly what true faith means.

To begin with, faith is an action of the mind. It's an attitude, a belief about something. In the context we're discussing it here, we accept by faith that, in spite of the wrong things we've done, God will put us in a right relationship with Himself. This does not mean, however, that our faith can be indifferent to the evil in our lives. True faith includes the following attitudes on our part:

- True faith says, I agree with God's judgment against evil. He hates it, and so do I.
- True faith agrees with God's judgment against the evil in *my* life. He hates it, and so do I.

Grace

- True faith makes a commitment to overcome sin, regardless of how difficult that may be.

Another word for what I've just described is *repentance*, which means to be sorry for the wrong things we've done. And this brings us to the relationship between faith and obedience.

While God doesn't require us to have actually *overcome* the wrong things in our lives before He will accept us and put us in a right relationship with Him, He does ask us to have the same attitude toward evil that He does. And not just evil in a general sense. It's easy enough to hate the evil deeds of the murderers, rapists, and thieves among us. But God wants us to hate *our own* evil. We may not have gained the victory over our personal evil, but we must *want* that victory; we must put ourselves *on the side* of victory. Then, even though we have not yet *gained* that victory, God treats us as though we *had*. That's what it means to be justified or put right with God *by faith*.

Now you can better understand the implication of what Jesus meant when He said to Johanna, "Neither do I condemn you." It's not that He was indifferent to her adultery. It's not that He was excusing the wrong she'd done. But He sensed that she was deeply repentant for what she'd done, so He applied His grace. He forgave her. He accepted her in spite of what she'd done. He gave her back her self-esteem, and He committed Himself to helping her live a better life in the future.

I pointed out in the previous chapter that many if not most of the crises that we face in life are the result of our own character defects. Thus, if we're going to improve our ability to handle crisis, and if we're going to reduce the number of crises in our lives, we must begin facing up to our character defects. But the moment we do that our self-esteem is threatened. That's why pride is such a hindrance to admitting our defects. Pride wants to preserve self-esteem at all costs, even if that means covering up the very things that are destroying our self-esteem in the first place.

But God has a solution for that. He says, I'll give you back your self-esteem in spite of all those defects in your character and the evil you've done because of them. I'll accept you right where you are, and then I'll help you overcome those defects and bad habits.

Grace and crisis

So what does all this have to do with preparing to deal with crisis?

Keep in mind that many of the crises in our lives are the result of our own character defects—defects that we love and are loathe to give up in spite of the turmoil they're creating for us. Even in the case of those crises that are no fault of our own whatsoever—such as a tornado that destroys our home or the plane crash that claims the life of a loved one—our character defects can keep us from handling them properly.

Grace works a profound spiritual change in our lives. It's God's first step in helping us to correct our character defects. Grace is especially important for people who feel profound shame and guilt over their wrong, dysfunctional behavior. For there's no way such people can hope to overcome their defects and sins as long as they believe God is angry with them for who they are and what they've done.

That's why grace—God's acceptance of us right where we are, with all our character defects and the evil behavior that arises out of them, is the first step in correcting them and preparing to handle the next major crisis in our lives.

---

[1]This story is recorded in John 8:1-11. With the exception of Jesus, we do not know the names of any of the people in this story. And, as an artist does with paint on canvass, I have imagined certain other details in order to make the story seem more real.

[2]Luke 10:38-42.

[3]Matthew 26:6-13.

[4]John 8:11.

[5]God doesn't want us to keep on sinning, but He knows that victory over sin is a process, not an event. He knows that character development is the work, not of a moment or a day, but of a lifetime.

[6]Every sin is a stupid mistake.

[7]Romans 3:28.

[8]Ephesians 2:8, 9.

Transformation

A drunk discovered the path to spiritual transformation.

A drunk? What does a drunk know about spirituality? More than you might think.

Bill Wilson became very successful at trading in the stock market back in the mid-1920s. As he put it, "Fortune threw money and applause my way. I had arrived. My judgment and ideas were followed by many to the tune of paper millions."[1] He and his wife lived sumptuously. They spent thousands of dollars on having a good time.

Unfortunately, alcohol was also an exhilarating part of Bill's life—and a growing problem. What had begun as a once-a-day "shot in the arm" became an all-day affair and sometimes continued most of the night. But as long as the stock market boomed, he was able to enjoy both the boom and the booze.

Then came October 24, 1929. Black Thursday. With tens of thousands of other speculators, he was wiped out. The boom was gone. The booze wasn't.

Transformation

Bill and his wife knocked around the United States and Canada for several years, experiencing varying degrees of success, but the financial trend was always downward. And the more the boom decreased, the more the booze increased. Eventually, Bill woke up to the fact that he had a problem with alcohol, and he promised his wife that he would never touch it again. However, as every addict knows, that promise, while sincere, was flawed. A few days later a friend offered him a drink, and he took it. And the next day and the next. He kept repeating the promise to his wife and vowing to himself that it would never happen again, but it always did. And each time he lost the battle he was filled with guilt, remorse, and a growing sense of hopelessness.

Eventually Bill ended up in a mental hospital for alcoholics. "It was a devastating blow to my pride," he later wrote. "I, who had thought so well of myself and my abilities, of my capacity to surmount obstacles, was cornered at last. Now I was to plunge into the dark, joining that endless procession of sots who had gone on before."

To say the least, Bill had a character defect, a spiritual flaw that was creating one crisis after the other in his life.

Unfortunately for Bill, back then the only solution for alcoholism that anyone knew about was either the insane asylum or the undertaker. "No words can tell of the loneliness and despair I found in that bitter morass of self-pity," Bill said.

"Quicksand stretched around me in all directions. I had met my match. Alcohol was my master."

Yet unbeknown to him at the time, he had actually taken the first step toward recovery. A friend was to show him the next.

Bill was sitting in his kitchen one day with a glass of alcohol in front of him when the phone rang. An old drinking pal asked if he could come over. This friend had been as much a drunk as Bill, if not worse. He too had been committed for alcohol insanity. Bill thought, *Good! Someone to share a drink with!* and promptly invited his friend over. But when he answered the door, his friend stood there, "fresh-skinned and glowing." As Bill would put it later, "There was something about his eyes. He was inexplicably different. What had happened?"

Bill offered his friend a drink. He refused. "What's all this about?" Bill asked. The friend's answer was very simple: "I've got religion."

Bill was stunned. Religion was the last thing he wanted to hear about right then. But his friend offered to share his experience if Bill cared to listen, and Bill was sufficiently impressed that he decided to hear him out. It came down to one thing: "My friend sat before me, and he made the point-blank declaration that God had done for him what he could not do for himself. Here sat a miracle directly across the kitchen table. He shouted great tidings. I saw that my friend was much more than inwardly reorganized. He was on a different footing. His roots grasped new soil."

But Bill had never been religious. Not that he was an atheist. He'd always believed in a power greater than himself. He believed that somehow there was design and purpose in the universe. But that's about where he and religion parted company. The word *God* aroused a certain antipathy in his mind, and he doubted whether that kind of God would be interested in helping him.

Bill's friend said his conception of God didn't matter and suggested that he give himself to God *just as he understood Him*. Bill had never thought of that, but he decided to give it a try. With his friend's help, he says, "I humbly offered myself to God, as I then understood Him, to do with me as He would. I placed myself unreservedly under His care and direction. I admitted for the first time that of myself I was nothing; that without Him I was lost. I ruthlessly faced my sins and became willing to have my new-found Friend take them away, root and branch. *I have not had a drink since.*"[2]

As you may know, Bill Wilson went on to found Alcoholics Anonymous—a spiritual program that has helped millions of people all over the world to break free of their addiction to alcohol. And people with many other addictions are also finding freedom through the spiritual principles of the Twelve Steps.

THE COMING GLOBAL CRISIS

You may not be any more religious than Bill was, and that's OK. But I hope you noticed that after turning his life over to God as he understood Him, *Bill never took another drink*. The key question for you and me is, What happened in Bill's mind that brought such a dramatic change? Here's what Bill said:

> The effect was electric. There was a sense of victory, followed by such a peace and serenity as I had never known. There was utter confidence. I felt lifted up, as though the great wind of a mountain top blew through and through. God comes to most men gradually, but His impact on me was sudden and profound.

Notice Bill's words: "A sense of victory," "peace and serenity," "felt lifted up," and a "sudden and profound" impact. That's a spiritual experience, in this case a transforming spiritual experience with God. I say "transforming," because through this experience Bill became in many ways a different person from what he had been up to that moment.

That's the spiritual change you and I need in order to begin overcoming those character defects that drag us from one crisis to the next. Let's talk about Bill's transforming experience for a moment.

Transformation

Foolish things suddenly make sense

Notice that what had seemed foolish to Bill before suddenly made perfectly good sense! This sudden enlightenment—what had seemed so odd suddenly shining as a bright truth—is one of the major characteristics of a transforming spiritual experience. And Bill Wilson is not an isolated case. Thousands, yes millions of people all over the world, have experienced the same thing. It's an "A-ha!" sort of thing—at first you don't see it . . . then suddenly you do. It's totally spiritual.

Let me illustrate.

Imagine yourself late one afternoon sitting all alone on a concrete slab that your state's park service has built near the top of a thousand-foot cliff. It's one of those "scenic viewpoints" that highway engineers kindly spend a little extra of the government's money on so that we can all enjoy a bit of nature's beauty. This particular viewpoint overlooks a valley filled with farms, pastures, barns, and homes. Trees line a creek that winds its way the length of the valley, and near the lower end of the creek is a mill on the edge of a small town.

Right now you're not paying attention to the farms, the creek, and the mill though. It's almost sundown, and the clouds are turning vibrant shades of pink, orange, and purple. With the green valley in the foreground and the blue sky as a backdrop, it's one of the most beautiful sunsets you've ever seen. In fact, the scene is so breathtaking that you're oblivious to the fact that someone is approaching until a tap-tap-tap on the concrete breaks your trance. Curious, you turn and see a young woman leading a man with a white cane in his hand.

"Oh, honey," the woman cries, "that's the most beautiful sunset I've ever seen! The pink and orange clouds are lined all the way around with the brightest gold from the setting sun!" She goes on and on exclaiming about the scene, and you're sitting there thinking, *Yes! Yes! Yes!*

Suddenly the man blurts out, "Awe, hon, let's get out of here. I haven't got time to waste on such foolishness."

"Oh, please, just a little longer," the young woman pleads. "It'll all be over in a few minutes and then we can leave."

"But I'm in a hurry," he snaps.

She leads him to a nearby park bench and turns him so he's facing away from it. "Here," she says in a sweet voice, "sit here just a few more minutes, and then we'll go."

"Oh, all right, all right, all right," the man grumbles. Leaning on his cane with one hand, he reaches back and feels for the bench with the other. "What's a sunset!" he mutters under his breath as he lowers his frame onto the wooden slats.

The young woman sighs and looks your way

with a slight shake of her head. The two of you exchange a glance and a smile. Then you both turn and keep on taking in the scene in front of you.

What's the problem here? Very simply, the blind man, lacking the ability to *see* the sunset, has absolutely no comprehension of it, and he can't possibly understand his companion's desire to stay and take it all in. To him it's all a huge waste of time. And until he gains the ability to see what she sees, there's no way the beauty of a sunset will ever make any sense to him whatsoever. He can choose to sit patiently or impatiently, but to his dying day he'll never understand, because with rare exception, blind people never gain the ability to see.

This little parable, if I may call it that, illustrates an important truth about a transforming encounter with God: You have to experience it to understand it. And once you've experienced it, you'll know forever that it's both true and wonderful, even while others around you are muttering about how foolish you are.

The good news is that this kind of spiritual encounter with God is open to everyone. Each of us has the capacity to "see." Whether we choose to is up to us and, of course, God respects our choice either way. (I wouldn't want a God who didn't, and I doubt you would either.) But the opportunity is always there, awaiting the time we need it.

Spiritual power

Another thing we learn about spirituality from Bill's experience is that a transforming encounter with God not only changes the way a person thinks; it gives him the power to do things that had been impossible to do before. In Bill's case, it gave him the victory over alcohol. *A transforming spiritual experience translates into spiritual power.* However, that spiritual power does not originate within us humans. It has to come from an external source. It has to come from God.

Let me illustrate again.

An engine is a block of steel that's been molded, cut, and drilled into just the right shape so it can work for us. Some engines carry us from place to place. Others lift heavy objects and move them around for us. Engines help us travel through water and fly through the air. Some even carry us out into space! We've invented all sorts of handy ways to use engines.

Every engine, sitting on its mounts, has the potential to do work—but by itself it can't do a thing. Before an engine can run, it has to be hooked up to a gas tank and a battery. The gasoline and the battery are two external energy sources, which, when introduced into the engine in just the right manner, give it the internal power it needs to run and do work for us.

In the same way, I propose to you that an external source of spiritual energy is available to every human being. And those who tap in to

Transformation

God's spiritual power also experience the spiritual insight that seems such a mystery, and even foolishness, to those on the outside.

From time to time most of us sense a need for this connection, and when things get desperate enough we may cry out for it. And, of course, we will receive it. But I propose to you that Jesus lived in that connection at all times. *And that same continual connection with God is available to you and me.* Many people say this experience is nonsense, but those who have experienced it know that it's real.

Bill Wilson experienced this connection with God, and that's what gave him the victory over alcohol. Up to that point, every one of his efforts to stop his destructive drinking had ended in failure, and in utter discouragement he had resigned himself to either the insane asylum or the undertaker. But notice what he said when his friend introduced him to God: "The effect was electric. There was a sense of victory, followed by such a peace and serenity as I had never known. There was utter confidence. I felt lifted up, as though the great wind of a mountain top blew through and through. God comes to most men gradually, but His impact on me was sudden and profound." And he concluded by saying, "I have not had a drink since."

Bill's battle with alcohol was actually a spiritual battle that he had tried for years to cope with in the strength of his own spirituality. But he discovered that alcohol was stronger than he was, and he needed an external source of spiritual power to deal with it. Once Bill plugged in to a source of spiritual power outside of himself, *he never took another drink.*

Some people may protest that it was all in Bill's head. Just mental gymnastics. Psychological manipulation.

Well and good. I'll be the first to admit that no one can prove in any scientific way that a spiritual experience of this sort originates with a God who lives in some distant part of the universe. Isn't it significant, though, that all over the world and in all cultures, people who put their faith in God have had an experience similar to Bill's? That says something about what *belief* in God can do in a person's life. Whether He exists or not, believing that He does and that He cares about us brings a transforming spiritual power into people's lives.

You know, of course, that I believe God *does* exist and that He *is* an external Source of spiritual power that we human beings can tap in to. I believe this because I believe the Bible, which claims to tell us about God. Even people who don't believe in God generally recognize that the Bible is one of the world's most influential spiritual books, so let's take a moment to see what the Bible has to say about this important topic.

What the Bible says about God's transforming spiritual power

"I am not ashamed of the gospel," the apostle Paul wrote to the Christians in Rome, "because *it is the power of God for the salvation of everyone who believes.*"[3] The "gospel" that Paul spoke of here is the hope of eternal life through Jesus Christ. And he said this gospel is the power of God for salvation. By "power of God," Paul means God's transforming spiritual power, which is available to everyone who believes. This power is external to us. We are not born with it. It does not reside within us naturally. We can only receive it.

Those who tap in to this power find their lives changed. As Paul said in another place, "Do not conform any longer to the pattern of this world, but *be transformed by the renewing of your mind.*"[4] God's power transforms the minds of those who receive it. They discover that habits and addictions that had enslaved them for years are broken. Their sullen tempers are subdued. Where they had been anxious about money, power, and position they now feel at peace. And it can happen to you. *If you access God's external spiritual power, it will transform your life.*

Because we can't see God's spiritual power with our eyes or touch it with our fingers, the Bible writers used metaphors to help us understand it. One of the best known is the "new birth."[5] That's actually a very good metaphor to illustrate the transformed spiritual life. We typically consider birth to be the beginning of a new physical life, which gives us the physical power to walk and run and jump and work and play. In the same way, the new birth is the beginning of a new spiritual life, which provides us with the power to accomplish mental, emotional, and spiritual feats that had been impossible for us to achieve before.

The new birth that we experience when we connect with God's spiritual power is the foundation of a spiritual experience with God. Everything else in our spiritual growth springs from that. That last point is so important that I'd like to repeat it:

> Everything else in our spiritual growth springs from
> this transforming spiritual experience with God
> that we call the "new birth."

According to the New Testament, this spiritual power especially comes to us through Jesus. And that does make sense, doesn't it, when you consider how Jesus treated people who were spiritually broken? Think back to Johanna in the previous chapter. Though she was a prostitute and an adulteress, Jesus treated her with respect. He saw beyond the external "facts in the case" to the spiritual need in her heart and mind. He forgave her and gave her hope for a better life in the future. Jesus is the kind of Spiritual Guide we all need! No wonder Paul said, "I can do all things through Christ who strengthens me."[6] Jesus is a source of external power that is available to each of us.

I propose that the most important spiritual preparation you can make for your next crisis is to bring God's transforming spiritual power into your life. Maybe you don't sense a need for that power right now. But who knows when a crisis may hit that leaves you "gasping for breath." God's transforming spiritual power will always be there for you when you need it.

---

[1]*Alcoholics Anonymous,* third edition (New York: Alcoholics Anonymous World Services, Inc., 1976), 3. All other quotations in Bill's story that follow are from this same source, pages 1-16.

[2]Italics supplied.

[3]Romans 1:16, italics supplied.

[4]Romans 12:2, italics supplied.

[5]John 3:3-5.

[6]Philippians 4:13, New King James Version.

CHAPTER 8

Faith

The film *Patch Adams* begins with Patch so depressed that he commits himself into a mental hospital. In the hospital he encounters a variety of strange people. One old man—Arthur Mendelson in the film—looks him intently in the eye, holds up four fingers, and says, "How many do you see?"

Patch looks at the old man for a moment, then says, "Four."

"Four!" Mendelson says as he walks away in disgust. "Four! Four! Four! Another idiot!"

A few days later Patch's curiosity gets the best of him. He goes into Mendelson's room and asks. "What's the answer?"

Mendelson tries to ignore him, but Patch persists. Finally the old man takes Patch's hand and holds it up with four fingers showing. Again he asks, "How many do you see?"

"Four," Patch says.

"No, no!" Mendelson protests. "You see what everyone else sees. You're focusing on the problem. Look beyond the fingers. Look at me."

Faith

Patch looks for a long time, and as his eyes come unfocused he sees double, and he says, "Eight!"

"A-ha!" Mendelson exclaims, and then he explains: "If you focus on the problem you can't see the solution. You've got to look beyond the problem."

These words will become a metaphor for Patch's life. However, one more event has to happen in the mental hospital before he's ready to leave and embark on the mission that will consume him for the rest of his life.

When Patch entered the mental hospital, he was placed in a room with an odd character named Rudy, who mostly sits at the head of his bed rocking back and forth as he complains loudly about the "squirrels" in the room. He's terrified of them. One night Patch is trying to sleep, but Rudy is rocking back and forth on his squeaky bed. "Lie down and go to sleep," Patch says impatiently, but Rudy can't because the "squirrels" are keeping him from going to the bathroom. Finally, in desperation, Patch gets up and says, "OK, where are the squirrels? Show me."

Rudy cringes on his bed, raises a finger, and points toward the foot of Patch's bed. "Over there," he says.

With deliberate slowness, Patch turns and looks over his shoulder. Then he sticks out the index finger of his right hand, points it at the "squirrel," and says "Bam!"

Rudy jumps, but Patch points his finger again and says "Bam!" Another squirrel is dead! Patch keeps shooting squirrels. "Bam! Bam! Bam!"

Now Patch has Rudy's attention! Soon Rudy is off his bed shooting squirrels along side of Patch. Patch grabs the edge of Rudy's bed and turns it on its side as a "bunker," and the two of them hide behind it as they continue their war on squirrels. "Bam! Bam! Bam!" Squirrels are "dying" all over the place!

At the height of the action, Patch yells, "It's safe to go into the bathroom!" Distracted by all the action and perhaps convinced that they really have killed the squirrels, Rudy ducks into the bathroom and closes the door. Patch leans with his back against the wall and listens. A moment later he hears the sound of "water" running into the toilet, and he lets the air out of his lungs in a huge sigh.

This story sounds ludicrous, but it has a tremendous point. Patch had a problem: Rudy's persistent rocking back and forth was keeping him awake. But the solution for Patch lay, not in trying to solve his own problem, but in looking beyond his problem and helping Rudy solve *his* problem. Patch had to get his mind off of the fact that Rudy was keeping him awake long enough to enter for a moment into Rudy's world and see the situation from Rudy's perspective. By helping Rudy solve *his* problem, Patch found the solution to his own.

Faith

The next morning Patch went into the medical director's office and said, "I'm leaving."

"You can't do that," the psychiatrist said.

"Oh yes I can," Patch replied. "I admitted myself."

"Why do you want to leave?" the doctor asked.

"Because I want to help people," Patch said. "Last night for the first time in my life I connected with another human being. I want to go out and help people." And he left.

A year or so later Patch enrolled in the medical training program at the University of Virginia. The rest of the film shows the unique and often crazy ways he found to connect with patients and help them see their world from a new perspective. In a children's ward he cut the end off a plastic ear syringe and stuck it on his nose. He put his feet in a couple of bed pans and clattered around the ward in his new "shoes." And the children loved it! An old woman confided in Patch that one of her life-long desires had been to "swim around" in a pool full of wet spaghetti, so he filled a large plastic swimming pool with wet spaghetti and threw her in it—to her utter delight.

The stoical medical director of the hospital was shocked at Patch's unorthodox methods, but Patch knew he was right, and he kept up his antics with patients. Half way through his medical training the frustrated medical director forbade him to ever enter the hospital again. Patch went to the dean of the school of medicine and got a reprieve. Finally, shortly before graduation, the medical director threw him out of the medical training program all together. Patch demanded a hearing before the state medical board, and the board reinstated him with a reprimand to the medical director to lighten up.

Faith

Why do I tell you this story? Because it's an excellent example of the topic of this chapter: Faith.

Patch Adams had two kinds of faith. First, he believed absolutely in the validity of his approach to patients. At first his fellow students thought he was a crackpot, and some of them refused to have anything to do with him. His arrogant roommate was convinced he was the world's greatest nerd. But Patch knew he was right, and he refused to be shaken from his convictions by either students or professors. And in the end he won. Eventually, even his roommate came around. One day he came to Patch and said, "I've got a patient that I've treated with the best medical knowledge available today, but I can't make her eat. This woman is going to die if she doesn't eat, but I can't make her eat. Patch, you can make her eat. Can you help me?"

Patch did. She's the woman he threw into the pool of spaghetti. And she got well!

Second, Patch had faith in himself; that he

could successfully carry out his philosophy of patient care. And again, he wasn't deterred by the fact that others didn't agree with him, or even that they thought he was foolish.

This book is about spirituality and spiritual solutions to the problems that create crises in our lives. Faith is a profoundly spiritual character trait. It's a trait we all need in order to succeed in life. Every successful person has Patch's two kinds of faith. Your philosophy of life may not be as original with you as Patch's view of patient care was, but that's not the point. Whatever your philosophy of life, and regardless of where you got it, you have to believe in it, and you have to believe in your ability to carry it out.

It's important to understand that faith always involves risk. That's because faith, in order to truly be faith, has to involve the unknown. Faith is a certainty both in your cause and in yourself that you are right, even though what you believe in has not been demonstrated. That's why the Bible says that faith is "being sure of what we hope for and certain of what we do not see."[1]

Before most people had even thought about light bulbs, Thomas Edison got the idea to make one. I'm told that Edison and his research associates conducted 3,000 experiments before they finally figured out the exact combination of gases in the bulb and the right combination of metals in the filament so that the bulb would glow without burning up. Half way through the R & D process a reporter came to the famous scientist and said, "Mr. Edison, you've conducted 1,500 experiments in your effort to perfect a light bulb, and so far you've failed every time. Don't you think you ought to just give up and admit that it's not possible to make a light bulb?"

Mr. Edison squared his shoulders, looked the reporter in the eye, and said, "Young man, I have not failed 1,500 times. I have successfully identified 1,500 ways that will not work to make a light bulb."

Mr. Edison had faith in his idea—that somewhere, somehow, it was possible to make a light bulb that worked. He also had faith in himself, that he could figure out how to do it. And he didn't allow other people's doubts to deter him from these convictions. He kept right on experimenting until he had developed a working light bulb.

This kind of faith is energizing. And the energy grows with each success. I know, because I've experienced it.

Fear

The opposite of faith is fear. This is sharply illustrated in one of Jesus' best-known parables. A man called in three of his servants and entrusted them with his wealth. To one he gave five talents of money, to another two talents, and to another one. Each man received what the master felt he was capable of handling. Then the master went on a long journey.

The men with five and two talents immediately invested their master's money, and soon they had doubled it. Investing money always involves a risk, but these men believed in the cause their master had entrusted to them, and they had confidence in their ability to handle the responsibility. So they took the risk, and they won. The one-talent man, however, went and buried his master's money in the ground.

Later the master returned and called his servants in to give an account of the responsibility he had charged them with. When the first two reported their success, the master commended them and gave them an additional responsibility. But the third man said, " 'I was afraid and went out and hid your talent in the ground. See, here is what belongs to you.' "[2]

"I was afraid."

The one-talent man wasn't sure that a profitable investment was possible. Even if it was for others, he knew *he* was not capable of making a profitable investment. He had no faith in the system, and he had no faith in himself, and because of these doubts he was afraid to take the risk that a proper investment of his master's money required.

Fear is a negative spiritual quality, and it is the great enemy of faith. In order to exercise faith, we must overcome our fears. Christians call the eleventh chapter of Hebrews the "faith chapter," because it reviews a number of Old Testament stories about faith in action, but it could also be called the "no fear chapter."

- At God's command, Noah built an ark to save himself and others from a flood. He had to overcome the fear that people might laugh at him for preparing for a flood that no one had seen. He had faith in God's command and his ability to carry it out.
- At God's command, Abraham went to a land he had never seen. To do that he had to overcome fear of the unknown. He had faith in God's command and his ability to carry it out.
- At God's command, Moses led Israel through the Red Sea, but to accomplish this feat they had to overcome the very normal fear of drowning! They had faith in God's command, and they risked drowning to carry it out.

Fear is the great enemy of faith. On the other hand, faith overcomes fear. If there's something you believe in very strongly but you're also afraid of it, take the risk. Launch out and do it. When you win, you'll have overcome your fear, and your faith in yourself and in your cause will be much stronger. And if at first you don't succeed, remember Thomas Edison's 3,000 experiments and keep trying.[3]

Faith

Faith in God

This brings us to another kind of faith that I would like to discuss with you in this chapter: Faith in God. There are two kinds. The first is simply the belief that God exists. Now no one has ever seen God. It's impossible to take the "God hypothesis" into the laboratory and test it. You see a stone fall to the ground, and you *know* that gravity exists, but there is no such compelling reason to believe in God's existence. All kinds of arguments have been devised to prove that He exists, the most common of which is probably the "design in nature." Those of us who believe in God may find the design-in-nature argument persuasive, but the agnostics and atheists among us are proof that it's far short of compelling.[4] Thus, in the end, we are left with belief—faith. The Bible states it succinctly: "Anyone who comes to [God] must *believe* that he exists."[5]

However, mere acceptance of the idea that God exists is pretty much a mental exercise. A deeper kind of faith in God is also possible. The question is, Can—or should—the idea of God's existence affect our lives in any practical sense? Plenty of people give mental assent to the idea of God's existence, then go about their business as if He didn't exist. On the other hand, multitudes have found that the idea of God's existence makes a powerful spiritual difference in their lives. But again, no one can prove this in any scientific sense. It's a matter of faith. That's why the Bible says that "anyone who comes to [God] must believe [both] that he exists *and* that he rewards those who earnestly seek him."[6]

The difference between these two kinds of faith is the difference between belief and trust. It's like the difference between knowing *about* the president of the United States (you've seen him on TV) and knowing him as a friend.

And so often, crisis seems crucial to experiencing this deeper kind of faith. As I have argued before in this book, crises are both a test of our faith and a springboard into future spiritual growth. Faith is one of the most important of life's spiritual qualities, and crises are both a test of our faith in God and a springboard into a deeper trust.

A good example of crisis as a springboard to a deeper faith is the alcoholic who "hits bottom." Alcohol may destroy his job, his family, or his finances. It may land him in jail. It may kill a loved one. Whatever the situation in the particular alcoholic's life, it's a crisis of major proportions—and it's also the best thing that could happen to him, because it has the potential to lead him or her to faith. Ever since Bill Wilson founded Alcoholics Anonymous in the late 1930s, alcoholics all over the world have been turning to God as the solution to their spiritual disease. Hitting bottom was their springboard to faith in God. It caused them to realize that only a greater power outside themselves could restore them to sanity.[7] Those who pursue this faith find that they are healed of the disease of alcoholism.

And the same principle works for any other character defect. *Faith in God is a powerful agent for spiritual change.*

On the other hand, crisis can also be a *test* of faith. People who have believed in God all their lives, perhaps even attended church since childhood, have found their faith severely tested when they came down with cancer or their house burned down or they got fired from their jobs. One of the most common responses to a crisis like that is "Where was God when . . . ?"

Their faith is being tested.

The issue is not whether such people believe God exists. The very question "Where was God when . . . ?" assumes that He does. The issue is whether they *trust* Him. The crisis reveals the genuineness of their claim to trust. It also launches them into a deeper trust in God.

Faith and salvation

Most religions of the world teach in one way or another that death is not the end, that we human beings have access to eternal life beyond the grave. Most religions also teach that this eternal life will be good—free of the suffering and imperfections that plague us in this life. And there's almost universal agreement that our present ills are the result of evil. Thus, most religions teach that in order to obtain eternal life in that good place beyond the grave we must deal with the evil that is a part of our experience in this life.

Another area of general agreement among the world's religions is that at its foundation, evil is individual and not just corporate. The problem is not just a few bad apples that spoil the rest of the barrel. Every apple is spoiled. Every human being is infected with evil. Christianity agrees. Paul declared that "all have sinned and fall short of the glory of God."[8]

Since the next life can't be good if it also is infected with evil, then evil people obviously must be excluded from that perfect paradise. But how can anyone qualify for that eternal life if we're all evil in this life? Again, nearly all religions agree that each person must deal with his or her evil in this life.

For many religions, the solution is to use this life learning how to be good. Our good deeds in the here and now demonstrate our worthiness to live eternally in the great beyond.

For Christianity, the solution to the problem of personal evil is quite different. Christianity begins by declaring the very opposite of what most other religions teach. It says that no one can qualify for eternal life by living a good life. Paul said it succinctly: "No one will be declared righteous in [God's] sight by observing the law."[9]

Faith

By "law," Paul probably meant the Ten Commandments, but in the broadest sense he meant all of God's requirements as outlined in the Bible. Simply stated, *our acceptance by God does not depend on learning to be good.*

Paul doesn't mean, of course, that we can live as we please or that obedience is irrelevant and disobedience doesn't matter. He means that God begins dealing with evil by accepting human beings right where they are, sins and warts and all. He does not demand that we reform our lives first. He does not require us to perform a certain number or quality of good deeds as a way to prove our goodness. As far as God is concerned, at the starting point, we humans don't have any goodness to offer. That's why He begins by accepting us just the way we are.

But God doesn't leave us where we are. At the same time that He accepts us, He also begins changing us on the inside. "Do not conform any longer to the pattern of this world," Paul said, "but be transformed by the renewing of your mind."[10] The transformation Paul speaks of involves our entire mind, character, and personality.

This is the new birth that I spoke about in the previous chapter. This new birth changes people at the deepest level of their minds and emotions. It's a spiritual eyesight that those who are spiritually blind—who have never experienced the new birth—can't possibly understand. Indeed, they'll think it's foolish!

But it's real, and it works a radical change. Where hatred existed, God begins planting love. Where doubt existed, He begins planting trust. Where fear existed, He begins planting peace. And that's the foolishness to those who have never experienced it. Their hatred, envy, and fear seem absolutely right. Never mind that these negative spiritual qualities are destroying their relationships and their happiness. They cling to these destructive feelings the way a drowning man clings to the sinking boat!

Yet even the sinking boat can be good news, because when the boat has finally disappeared under the water, some people will turn to the only other Source of help that's available: God. And the good news is that God doesn't demand that we swim to shore and start living right before He'll extend a helping hand. God reaches down, lifts us out of the water, and places us on dry ground first. Then He helps us to live a new and better life.

And God guarantees us eternal life in the hereafter from the very first moment that we turn to Him for help!

That, in a nutshell, is the Christian solution to the problem of evil, how evil people can become acceptable to God, and how they can qualify for eternal life beyond the grave. And a single word summarizes it all: Grace. The same grace Jesus extended to Johanna in spite of the fact that she had just committed adultery.

Faith

The question is, Do you and I believe in God's grace? Do we really believe He cares about us in spite of the wrong things we've done?

Faith says Yes! And that can be tough. Because most of us have enough uncertainty about our relationship with God to wonder whether He really *does* accept us just as we are, regardless of how evil we may have been. Pile on top of this the low self-esteem that some of us received as a legacy from our past, and faith in God's gracious acceptance of us right where we are, warts and all, becomes a tremendous challenge.

But remember the nature of faith: It believes in spite of challenges. Thomas Edison believed absolutely that a working light bulb could be made. He had confidence in his ability to figure out how, and he maintained that belief in spite of the doubts of newspaper reporters and skeptics. Patch Adams believed absolutely in his philosophy of treating patients, and he refused to be turned from that confidence by the ridicule of his fellow students and the opposition of the medical faculty.

Challenges to faith may come from outside ourselves, such as when unbelieving relatives or friends chide us for having "gotten religion." But just as often these challenges originate within. We feel unworthy of God's gracious acceptance of us right where we are. We feel that somehow, even if it's in a small way, we must "make it up" to God before He'll accept us. We think we have to turn our lives around and at least make a *start* at right living. Then maybe He'll relent and give us a bit of help.

But the Bible turns that argument around 180 degrees. According to the Bible, *God accepts us first,* regardless of how evil we have been, and *then* we start on the business of reforming our lives. Christians do not place faith in their ability to *deserve* God's acceptance by anything they do. They place their faith in God's grace—the idea that God will accept them just as they are. The whole point of the New Testament teaching about salvation is that eternal life is granted to those who place their trust in God. That's why Paul said that "a man is justified [or saved] by faith apart from observing the law."[11]

In our story a couple of chapters back, there was nothing that Johanna, given the facts her accusers brought against her, could have done to merit Christ's acceptance. No pledge to reform, regardless of how sincere or how faithfully kept, could change what she had already *done*. She *had* committed adultery, and according to the Law she *did* deserve to die. Jesus' treatment of her at that moment is a perfect picture of God's grace, of His acceptance of evil people right where they are.

But we must *believe* that's how He treats us. I must put absolute trust in the fact that He will treat *me* that way. You must place absolute confidence in the fact that He will treat *you* that way.

Faith

A number of years ago I made an hour-long presentation on this topic at a large Christian convocation. When I was through a woman came up to me. She was looking at the floor, and in a very quiet voice she said, "Is it true, Pastor Moore? Is it really true?"

I looked at this woman, and I said, "Yes, sister, what I have told you really is true."

She kept her face to the floor, and she shook her head, and she said, "I can't believe it. I just can't believe it."

This woman's faith was very imperfect. Fortunately, Jesus declared that faith the size of a grain of mustard seed—one of the smallest of all seeds—is enough to move mountains. A gracious God knows this woman's heart, the struggle she was going through to believe, and the extent to which she *could* believe. It's not for me to pass judgment on her standing with God. But I can say that her unbelief, if not a deterrent to her salvation, was a hindrance to her enjoyment of her relationship with God to the fullest extent. And it was definitely a hindrance to faith's accomplishing its full work in her life.

This book is about how to deal with crisis. Earlier in this chapter I said that faith in God is a powerful agent for spiritual change. It's a powerful agent for bringing about those spiritual changes in your life that will make it possible for you to handle crises successfully. So if you believe in God and trust that He accepts you right where you are, the next question is, How will He work with you to bring about those changes? How can you and He work together to develop positive character traits in your life so that the next time you are faced with a major crisis you can handle it even more successfully than you did the last one?

Let's talk about that in the next chapter.

---

[1]Hebrews 11:1.

[2]This story is recorded in Matthew 25:14-30.

[3]One word of caution: If your vision costs money to develop, before you begin you should be sure you have the financial resources to see it through to completion or that you set a limit on how much you can afford to lose in case you run out of money before you reach your goal. Also, any goal that would seriously jeopardize your health or your important relationships may not be worth the cost.

[4]A compelling argument is one that is so convincing that everyone will agree it has to be correct. No reasonable person can argue against it. An example is the statement that an object that is released above the ground will fall.

[5]Hebrews 11:6, italics supplied.

[6]Ibid., italics supplied.

[7]Step One of the Twelve Steps of Alcoholics Anonymous says, "We admitted we were powerless over alcohol—that our lives had become unmanageable." Step Two says, "Came to believe that a power greater than ourselves could restore us to sanity."

[8]Romans 3:23.

[9]Romans 3:20.

[10]Romans 12:2.

[11]Romans 3:28.

CHAPTER

Performance

Please read the following three letters and then ask yourself what advice you'd give the people who wrote them. The first letter was written back in the late 1980s to the therapist at a codependency treatment center:

> I've been an addict since the age of 13. I have two younger sisters and I had two younger brothers who died due to the hell that comes from alcohol and drugs. My father also died of the same hell. My mother, who I believe was bordering on insanity due to alcohol, has been living virtually homeless.
>
> My own drinking and drug abuse are getting worse. I've been experimenting with cocaine, smoking, and shooting. This past weekend I spent $75.00—our trailer lot rent money—on cocaine. I make $5.75 an hour, and that's a big chunk out of my paycheck.

Each time after I use and drink, I tell myself, my wife, my older son, and the Lord, that I'm sorry and that I want to stop. I want each time to be the last, but it never is. Only a month or so and I fall again.

My wife, along with other people who care, keeps telling me the only way to overcome this is through total dependence on Jesus. My wife is typing this letter for me and is asking me what else I want to say, but my mind is so confused I can't think right now what else to say, except, can you help me?

This next letter was published several years ago in the "Letters" section of a Christian youth magazine:

Just what is the solution when one has asked for forgiveness and made his confession, is willing to forsake his sins, has prayed earnestly, and consecrated himself to God only to find himself falling right back into sin?

Somewhere a vital link in the chain of becoming like Christ is missing for me. Has anyone who has trod the road ahead found the answer, the really workable solution that results, at the close of the day, in triumphant, heart-felt praise to such a Friend who could do so much for you? I'm all for 'victory to victory,' but HOW?

The third letter was written by the apostle Paul almost 2,000 years ago to the Christians in Rome:

I do not understand what I do. For what I want to do I do not do, but what I hate I do. And if I do what I do not want to do, I agree that the law is good. As it is, it is no longer I myself who do it, but it is sin living in me. I know that nothing good lives in me, that is, in my sinful nature. For I have the desire to do what is good, but I cannot carry it out. For what I do is not the good I want to do; no, the evil I do not want to do—this I keep on doing. Now if I do what I do not want to do, it is no longer I who do it, but it is sin living in me that does it.

So I find this law at work: When I want to do good, evil is right there with me. For in my inner being I delight in God's law; but I see another law at work in the members of my body, waging war against the law of my mind and making me a prisoner of the law of sin at work within my members. What a

wretched man I am! Who will rescue
me from this body of death?[1]

By their own admission, each of these people
was doing things that violated their conscience.
Their performance did not match their convictions. Each one was desperate to stop doing what
they knew to be wrong—but they couldn't. To
put it in religious terms, they couldn't stop sinning. This is an extremely common problem.
Here's how the Alcoholics Anonymous book
titled *Alcoholics Anonymous* (the so-called "Big
Book") describes it:

> The fact is that most alcoholics, for
> reasons yet obscure, have lost the
> power of choice in drink. Our so-called
> will power becomes practically nonex-
> istent. We are unable, at certain times,
> to bring into our consciousness with
> sufficient force the memory of the suf-
> fering and humiliation of even a week
> or a month ago. *We are without defense
> against the first drink.*[2]

It goes without saying that alcoholism creates
huge crises in the lives of its victims. It destroys
health, homes, and careers. And what's true of
alcoholism is true of ten thousand other bad
habits that we humans manage to get ourselves
addicted to.

Performance

So how can we get our performance to match up with our convictions of right and wrong? Alcoholics Anonymous has discovered the solution, or perhaps more correctly, has rediscovered it, because the solution is actually very ancient. The Bible started talking about it 3,500 years ago. It's the spirituality we've been discussing in the last four chapters:

> **Insight**—breaking out of denial
> **Grace**—acceptance by God
> **Transformation**—a redirection of our mind and emotions
> **Faith**—confidence that victory over our bad habits is possible for us

The people who wrote the letters I quoted didn't need insight into the fact that they had a problem. They *knew* they had a problem. What they didn't know was how to get *out* of the problem. Which is another way of saying that we human beings can get ourselves into crises that we can't back out of. This is particularly true of those crises that we bring on ourselves by our own bad habits and addictions. Even if we manage to extricate ourselves from the immediate cause of our distress (the credit card junkie figures out a way to pay this month's bills) the underlying cause continues to plague us (he charges another credit card to the max next month). And the wrong behavior will continue to plague us until we get to the root of the problem.

I'd like to suggest six things you can do to deal with the underlying cause of the crises in your life.

1. Seek grace

The very first step in changing your behavior is to seek God's grace. And the reason is very simple. One of the driving forces behind addiction is shame, and *there is no way you can overcome your bad habits as long as you are covered up with guilt and shame over them*. But when you know that God has forgiven you, that He is your Friend, and that He accepts you just as you are, you can let go of the guilt and shame.

Keep in mind, of course, that you can't claim God's forgiveness without a corresponding commitment to deal with the defects in your character. As I pointed out in the chapter on grace, God does not require that you actually overcome your bad habits and addictions before He will grant you His grace and forgiveness, but He's not interested in playing games with you. Did you notice how desperate for victory the three individuals in our introductory letters were? Sure, they were frustrated, but *they were serious about dealing with their addictions*. That's the attitude God is looking for. As long as you and I are serious about overcoming our bad habits, we can count on Him to accept us right where we are and to support us as we move toward victory.

So how can you obtain God's forgiveness and grace? Just say this prayer:

> God, this defect in my character keeps getting me in trouble, and I want to overcome it, but I don't know how. Please forgive me for the mistakes it's caused me to make in the past, and lead me to victory in the future.

Some people say that even after they've asked God to forgive them, they still feel guilty. That's not genuine guilt. It's caused by our shame, which we *interpret* as guilt. It's only a feeling and not an indication that God rejects us.

2. Seek transformation

I've stressed in this book that our defective behavior is rooted in our defective character traits. If we are spiritually flawed on the inside— if we have dysfunctional attitudes and emotions—these are bound to translate into defective behavior on the outside. Some religious people clench their fists and grit their teeth and try not to *do* certain things they consider to be wrong. Unfortunately, while I am sympathetic with their desire to live a moral life, they will almost certainly fail to gain the victory over their bad habits if all they're doing is clenching their fists and gritting their teeth.

THE COMING GLOBAL CRISIS

I'm not saying that clenching the fists and gritting the teeth is invariably a wrong approach to overcoming a bad habit. I'm only saying it's not the place to begin. The starting point *must* be a change on the inside. And on that score I have both bad news and good news to share with you.

The bad news is this: *You can't change your own wrong desires*. If you have a problem with a bad temper, you can grind your teeth down to your gums, but you won't succeed in changing your anger. If you are struggling with a food or sexual addiction, you can clench your fists till your fingernails pop out on the tops of your hands, but you won't be able to get rid of those wrong desires. Alcoholics Anonymous has discovered this, and what people have found to be true of alcohol addiction is true of every other besetting sin and addiction that we struggle with. Here's how Alcoholics Anonymous puts it:

> Our sponsors declared that we were the victims of a mental obsession so subtly powerful that no amount of *human will power* could break it.[3]

An obsession is simply a desire that you and I can't make go away. Our will power is not strong enough to do it. That's why we stay locked in the behavior that everyone else can see is destroying us. Often, even we can see that this habit is destroying us, but *we can't say No!* And the reason is that regardless of how much we may want to stop *doing* it, the desire keeps burning inside of us until we finally break over and do it anyway.

We have to have outside help.

Which is where the good news comes in: We can't change our own wrong desires, but *God can*. And His help is literally only a prayer away. Here's the prayer I suggest you say:

God, I'm powerless over this wrong desire. Please remove it, and replace it with a desire for what's right.

This is a powerful prayer, and I can assure you from personal experience that it works. If you keep saying it, the addictive desire will diminish.

3. Seek God's power to resist

There's one important point to keep in mind, though, about God's work on your dysfunctional desires: Emotions fade gradually, and God does not necessarily violate that principle when He changes your wrong desires.

Let's say, for example, that you're burning-up mad at Jane over something you think she did. You grind your teeth for several minutes to keep from exploding, and all the while the pressure inside of you is building. Then a friend points out to you that the problem was the result of circumstances beyond anyone's control. You now have a reasonable explanation for what happened, which lets Jane off the hook. But what about your anger? The adrenaline is in your system, and it's going to take you several minutes to cool down.

So if emotions fade gradually, what happens while the desire is fading? Here's where a lot of people get in trouble. Because they still *feel* like doing it, they conclude that God didn't answer their prayer for freedom from the desire, so they go ahead and "do it." But of course, that only intensifies their guilt.

What's the solution to this problem? It's called "white-knuckling it"—a strategy that every addict who is successful in his recovery is familiar with. White-knuckling it means to clench the fists, grit the teeth, and abstain from the behavior even though you feel like doing it.

However, I need to warn you that white-knuckling it is only a temporary strategy to use while the defective desire is fading. It does not work as a permanent strategy for avoiding the dysfunctional behavior, and even if it did, gritting the teeth and clenching the fists to keep the lid clamped on a burning desire is a miserable way to live.

White-knuckling it is very painful to do when the desire to indulge in your favorite bad habit is raging inside of you. That's why you need God's help not only to remove the wrong desire but also to give you the power to keep from acting on it while the desire is fading. And there's a good prayer for that, too:

God, please remove this wrong desire, and give me the power to not act on it right now.

Notice that this prayer begins with a request for God to remove the wrong desire. It's important to always begin there, but then to move immediately to the request for power not to act on it *right now*. God may not remove the wrong desire *right now*, but He will give you the power not to act on it *right now*.

The Bible summarizes all of this in just one short sentence: "I can *do* everything through him [God] who gives me strength."[4] All it takes is that simple prayer to access God's power to keep from "doing it" while He's removing the wrong desire.

4. Seek understanding

One of the most helpful ways I've found for overcoming a bad habit is to learn all I can about it. Scores of books are available on nearly every form of addiction. These books were written either by people who struggled with these issues themselves or by professionals who worked with those who were struggling.

Reading these books has helped me in several ways. First, it shows me that I'm not alone in my struggle. Others have been through it too, and if they conquered, so can I. And the authors of these books nearly always give lots of practical suggestions for dealing with the problem.

I've also discovered that just learning about my character defect removes some of my fear of it. And since fear is one of the things that keeps me obsessing, the more I learn about the issue, the easier the obsession is to deal with, and consequently, the easier it is to overcome the bad habit or addiction.

Finding these books is quite easy. If you have a computer with Internet access, look them up on your favorite bookstore web site. They all have a browse feature. Type in words related to the issue you're struggling with, and their computer will search for books on that topic and display them for you. Also, most bookstores carry these books in a section labeled "Recovery." Look for a book on your issue and read it. If you find several, read them all. I also suggest that you read everything you can about addiction and co-dependence.

5. Seek a spiritual mentor

One of the most effective ways I've found to deal with a habit I'm trying to shake off is to share the problem with someone who is willing to work through the issue with me. This strategy is especially helpful if the individual I work with has dealt with the same issue himself.

I need to warn you, though, that talking to someone else about the problem you're struggling with will probably seem difficult at first. We often feel intense shame over our character defects, particularly those that involve an issue such as sexual addiction or an anger-abuse addiction that society tends to frown on. That's the reason for the *anonymous* in Alcoholics Anonymous (or any other type of Twelve-Step program). Anonymity provides addicts with a safe place to go for help. If a Twelve-Step program for your addiction exists near your home, by all means attend it regularly.

But to get back to the topic of this section, you will find it helpful to find a spiritual mentor—what Twelve-Step groups call a "sponsor"—to work with you as you seek to overcome the character defect that is driving you into one crisis after another.

Many sponsors of addicts in Twelve-Step programs encourage the addict to call them when the desire to "do it" gets overwhelming. Some even go so far as to encourage the addict to call them in the middle of the night if necessary. The addict and the sponsor then talk the issue through until the addict feels able to handle the problem alone.

One caution, though. Be sure to choose a spiritual mentor who is of the same gender as yourself: men talk to men, women talk to women.

6. Seek patience

Many people become very discouraged when they fall for the same temptation day after day. They don't understand that we human beings seldom overcome a bad habit on the first try.[5] It takes time and a good bit of hard work to bend the character around so that it no longer produces the wrong behavior.

Part of the problem is that we live in a society that expects instant results. If something's wrong with the car or the computer, we're accustomed to taking it to the repair shop and picking it up all fixed a couple of days later. And we think the same should apply to our character development. Why can't God just fix it for us once and for all so we don't have to mess with it? Because God's way is to provide the tools and let us do the actual character development. And we need to give ourselves time for the character change to happen.

That means we need patience.

The workbook *The Twelve Steps: A Spiritual Journey* includes a couple of statements by recovering addicts that have helped me to understand this:

It is foolish not to anticipate relapses.[6]

It is wise to be gentle with ourselves and remember that it took a lifetime to develop these habits. It is not real-

istic to expect them to disappear over-
night.[7]

This principle is especially important for those
to remember who tend to punish themselves
with guilt every time they have a slip. Religious
people in particular tend to have this problem,
because they think God surely must be angry
with them for what they have just done. Here's
where it's helpful to remember the story of
Johanna that we discussed several chapters
back. Do you remember the last thing Jesus said
to her? " 'Neither do I condemn you. . . . Go now
and leave your life of sin.' "[8]

Two points in particular are important to remember from these words. First, Jesus acknowledged that what she'd done was wrong. He said,
in effect, "What you did keeps getting you in
trouble, so stop doing it." God never lowers His
standard of right and wrong to accommodate our
weaknesses. If He did, we would no longer have
a goal to strive for.

But Jesus also said, "Neither do I condemn
you." While He refused to lower the standard,
He recognized that she was a struggling human
being who hadn't yet overcome all her bad habits and addictions. In spite of the fact that she'd
just "done it" again, He was willing to accept her
right where she was and encourage her to keep
trying.

And that's how God deals with you when

you've just "done it" again. He takes you by the hand (symbolically, you understand) and says, "I know you just slipped and fell, but I also know that you still *want* to overcome this bad habit, so let Me help you learn how."

Do you remember the story of Thomas Edison? He failed 3,000 times before he finally perfected the light bulb. But did he really fail those 3,000 times? Not at all. Each so-called failure was actually a learning experience by which he taught himself how to make a light bulb.

The same can be true with your so-called failures. Treat each one as a learning experience. Ask yourself, What was going through my mind just before I slipped? What was I feeling? Did I seek God's help? Did I try to prevent the wrong behavior before asking God to change my desire? What might I do differently next time that would produce a different result? When you do this, you are experimenting with your spiritual life. You might call it "experimental spirituality" or "experimental religion."

So be patient. Give yourself a break. Cut yourself some slack. God doesn't demand instant victory of you. Why should you demand it of yourself?

I know these suggestions for overcoming bad habits and character defects work, because I've made significant progress on my own character defects by using them. I don't mean that they are easy to implement, because some of them can be really tough—like clenching your fists and gritting your teeth to keep from doing it while the desire is fading. But I find that when I do these things, my defects slip away a little at a time.

I also know that these suggestions have worked for many others, and I know they'll work for you. And as your character slowly bends around into increasing spiritual health, you are preparing yourself for the next major crisis in your life, including the big one that's going to hit the world one of these days.

---

[1]Romans 7:15-24.

[2]*Alcoholics Anonymous* (the "Big Book"), third edition (New York: Alcoholic World Services, 1976), 24, italics supplied .

[3]*The Twelve Steps and the Twelve Traditions*, (New York: Alcoholics Anonymous World Services, 1996), 22, italics supplied .

[4]Philippians 4:13, italics supplied .

[5]We've all heard of the cigarette smoker who threw away his pack and never wanted another one. But for every smoker like that there are a hundred who struggled for a year or five years before they finally gained the victory over tobacco.

[6]*The Twelve Steps: A Spiritual Journey* (San Diego: RPI Publishing, Inc., 1994), 26.

[7]Ibid., 90.

[8]John 8:11.

CHAPTER

Today

There's an interesting story in the Bible about a king of Israel—Hezekiah was his name—who got sick one day with a boil. Back then preachers did what they still do today when their parishioners get sick: They called on them. And in this case the preacher was the prophet Isaiah. But this wasn't your ordinary hospital visit. God instructed Isaiah to go to the king and say to him, " 'Put your house in order, because you are going to die.' "[1]

Talk about a crisis!

The Bible says Hezekiah turned his face to the wall and wept bitterly. (I'm sure we can all understand why!) As he was facing the wall the king prayed, " 'Remember, O Lord, how I have walked before you faithfully and with whole-hearted devotion and have done what is good in your eyes.' "

Isaiah hadn't even gotten past the middle court on his way out of the king's palace when God spoke to him again: " 'Go back and tell Hezekiah, . . . "I will heal you. . . . I will add fifteen years to your life." ' "

The bad news suddenly became wonderfully good news!

At the moment, yes. But think about this: As the years went by: one, two, three, the king could also count backwards: fifteen, fourteen, thirteen. That's not too bad when you're up in those high numbers. But how would you like to know that you had three, then two, then *just one year to live*. Then eleven months, ten months, nine months, down to *three, two, and one*.

Not so good after all!

I don't know about you, but I'd just as soon not know the date of my demise. For that matter, I'd just as soon not know in advance what the next major crisis in my life will be or when it will hit.

I asked Lois if she'd have wanted to know about that dog attack ahead of time.

"You bet," she said. "I'd have taken a different road!"

"Oh, no," I said. "You couldn't have prevented it. You would just have known it was coming. Would you have wanted to know about it ahead of time?"

"No way!" she said.

That's how it is with us human beings, isn't it? If we could prevent our next crisis—take steps to avoid it altogether—then, like Lois, we'd all say, "Sure! Tell me more!" But if there's no way to prevent it, we'd just as soon not know about our next crisis till it happens.

Here's the good news, though: You can *prepare* for your next crisis even though you don't *know* about it ahead of time.

A large cluster of tornadoes hit Oklahoma in the summer of 1999. I remember reading in my newspaper about a woman who, several years earlier, had turned one of the closets in her home into a storm shelter by building a cinderblock wall around it. When she and her family heard the tornado warning on their TV, they all hid in the storm shelter. The house around them was demolished, but they survived just fine.

This woman had no idea when—or even whether—a tornado would destroy her home, but she prepared ahead of time for the possibility.

In the same way, *you can prepare ahead of time for every single crisis you'll ever face*.

Spiritually, I mean.

For spiritual preparation is the most important preparation any of us can make. The woman who built a storm shelter was able to save her life and the life of her family members, but after the tornado they still had to deal with the crisis of a demolished house. I'm sure they had taken out storm insurance ahead of time, but no insurance company in the world could have protected this woman against the trauma of losing everything she owned and having to rebuild her house from scratch. The only advance preparation she could make for that part of the crisis was spiritual—the ability to survive without going to pieces.

It would have been impossible for this woman to build her storm shelter *after* hearing that the storm was on the way. And there's no way you and I can prepare spiritually for our next crisis *after* it's upon us. We have to do that ahead of time.

Today.

And tomorrow, and the next day, and the next, and the next.

Spiritual preparation takes time. It comes in tiny steps. From one day to the next you may wonder whether your efforts at spiritual change are even making a difference. Usually, though, from one month to the next, and certainly from one year to the next, you'll see those changes.

What about the global crisis that the book of Revelation says is coming on the world someday? Even if you agree with me that it's going to happen, please don't be frightened about it, because that wasn't God's intention in telling us about it. He told us so that we can prepare for it ahead of time.

Spiritually, I mean.

I can't tell you whether the coming global crisis will happen in your lifetime and mine. But I can assure you that if you're prepared for that one, you'll be ready for every other crisis that comes into your life between now and then.

THE COMING GLOBAL CRISIS

So now that you've finished reading this book, why not go back over it and create a plan of action?

- Ask God to show you the spiritual defects in your life that would cause you to mishandle your next personal crisis.
- Ask Him to help you understand His grace, which keeps you in His care during the time you're overcoming your character defects.
- Ask Him to place His transforming spiritual power in your life that will remove your wrong desires and replace them with a desire for what's right.
- Ask Him to give you the faith that these changes really *can* happen in *your* life.
- Ask Him to help your behavior to slowly bend around to match your desire and your efforts for change.

And what better time is there to start than—

Today!

---

[1]This story is recorded in 2 Kings 20:1-6.

If you enjoyed this book . . .

and would like to receive information about other books from Pacific Press, call **1-800-765-6955** for a **FREE** catalog, or visit our online bookstore at www.ABCASAP.com.

If you would like a **FREE** set of Bible study guides, phone toll free: **1-888-456-7933**, or write to: DISCOVER, Box 53055, Los Angeles, CA, 90053.